What Other People Are Saying

Whether presented in person or in her new book, Colleen Rickenbacher's message is universal. Her ideas are adaptable from an everyday business dinner to a meeting with a four-star general. Colleen's material has been not only informative and educational for our cheerleaders but also fun! We love her enthusiasm and zeal for her topics and her interactive presentations. This book is sure to be a winner!

—Kelli McGonagill Finglass
Director, Dallas Cowboys Cheerleaders
Irving, Texas

Psst! Your manners are showing! Even with today's more casual workplace, it's imperative that we still "mind our manners." And Colleen Rickenbacher, who personifies every facet of being the best in business, is a great teacher. Her timely book is clear and precise, her message refreshing. So enjoy the pleasant journey to being on your best business behavior!

—Edward E. Scannell, CMP, CSP
Co-author "Games Trainers Play" McGraw-Hill series
Director, Center for Professional Development and
Training—Scottsdale, Arizona

I had the pleasure of having Colleen Rickenbacher as the keynote speaker at our "Celebrating Women in the Workplace" event, where she shared many of the things addressed in her book. We found these suggestions to be a must-have for all women—single, married, widowed, housewife, mother, career woman. Colleen's energetic and enthusiastic way of communicating the information makes it fun and exciting to learn how to be at our best with confidence.

—Lindsay Roberts
First Lady of Oral Roberts University
Tulsa, Oklahoma

Colleen Rickenbacker's pragmatic and inspiring book is a treasure box full of great advice and golden nuggets. Rickenbacher's book reminds us that our true purpose is to serve each other. It is for people everywhere who count their blessings, thereby creating a positive effect for all lives they touch.

—Dee Simmons
Chairman and Founder
Ultimate Living International, Inc.
Dallas, Texas

BE ON YOUR BEST
BUSINESS
BEHAVIOR

BE ON YOUR BEST
BUSINESS
BEHAVIOR

HOW TO AVOID SOCIAL
AND PROFESSIONAL FAUX PAS

WHEN DINING, TRAVELING, CONVERSING,
AND ENTERTAINING

COLLEEN A. RICKENBACHER, CMP, CSEP

Brown Books Publishing Group
Dallas, Texas

Cover photograph: Nick Dolding/Getty Images

Manufactured in the United States of America.

For information, please contact:
Brown Books Publishing Group
16200 North Dallas Parkway, Suite 170
Dallas, Texas 75248
www.brownbooks.com
972-381-0009

ISBN 0-9713265-6-8
LCCN 2004101934
2 3 4 5 6 7 8 9 10

Dedication

To my family . . .
. . . for being so wonderful and
keeping my feet on the ground.

Contents

●●●●●●●

Dedication vii

Acknowledgments xi

Introduction xiii

ONE–Looking Your Best for Business I

TWO–Mastering Communication Technology 9

THREE–Behaving Professionally in the Workplace 17

FOUR–Networking: How to Work a Room .21

FIVE–Dining and Table Etiquette 31

SIX–Negotiating the Tabletop 43

SEVEN–Hosting and Attending Business Meals 55

EIGHT–Handling Difficult Foods 67

NINE–Working in a Home Office 79

TEN–Packing for Business Travel 95

ELEVEN–Being Safe at Home and on the Road 117

TWELVE–Tipping Guidelines 129

THIRTEEN–Business Entertainment. Gifts. and RSVPs 135

Reading List 145

About the Author 147

Acknowledgments

Thanks to Laurie Sprouse, CITE, DMCP, CMP, Ultimate Ventures, Inc. Dallas, Texas, for her packing list adapted for Chapter 10.

Also appreciation goes to the Dallas Police Department and National Fire Protection Association for background for Chapter 11.

Finally, Brown Books' staff and owner Milli Brown provided professional expertise in making this book reflect my message and the quality I espouse.

Thank you all.

Introduction

●●●●●●●

It's funny how certain people and events came together to cause me to write this book. It started about nine years ago when I was asked to do my first "Working Out of a Virtual/Home Office" presentation. I loved doing the session and people enjoyed learning from it. Then I was asked to do a presentation about dining etiquette. I had no idea how to do a professional presentation on etiquette, so I bought lots of reference books and watched programs on the topic before I did my presentation. And, again, it was useful to the audience. Eventually, opportunities came for presentations about networking, professional image, and other topics. So with Sherry Andrus, of the Dallas Convention & Visitors Bureau, and Meeting Professionals International giving me speaking opportunities, unknowingly, I was starting my book.

Then not long ago I walked into the store where I buy my clothing and Zary Tarjan, my salesperson, introduced me to another of her customers, Dee Simmons. That introduction changed things. Dee is a national spokesperson for Making Memories Breast Cancer Foundation and is a frequent guest on *Make Your Day Count,* a television show that Lindsay Roberts hosts from Oral Roberts University. It is a great show and reminds me of *The View* and *Oprah,* all rolled into one. Shown daily on satellite television, it includes the spiritual aspects of life. Dee contacted Lindsay and I was asked to be a guest on the show. I gave Lindsay handouts from the presentations I had done about dining etiquette, dressing professionally and networking and her audience began writing to request my book.

I really didn't have a book, but now I had a reason to put all my handouts together into a handy, practical reference. With the encouragement and push of my friends Hattie Hill and Betty Garrett and assistance from Linda Chandler, it all started to come together.

So to all these people, I say thank you for pushing me to finally make a dream come true to complete this book. And last, but not least, my loving thanks to my husband Steve for letting me stay in my office all hours of the day and night to finish it, and to my daughter Andrea, and my dear friend Mike Hileman for listening to me talk constantly about each chapter.

Enjoy the book. You may disagree with some ideas and that's fine. My goal is to provide practical suggestions and a starting point. If you have questions or concerns in any of these areas, contact me through my Web site, www.colleenrickenbacher.com. Who knows? Maybe your reactions will fuel my next book—*Be On Your Best Cultural Behavior!*

ONE

Looking Your Best for Business

• • • • • • •

Did you know you have only ten seconds to make a good first impression? It may not seem fair, but your appearance speaks for you before you can express your thoughts. What you wear influences others and can make you feel more confident and in control. Focus on being appropriately dressed every day. That client you've been courting for months may suddenly have an open lunch date, and you'll need to be ready on a moment's notice.

Successful Dressing and Image

- Wear appropriate clothes for each occasion. Respect dress codes. If you are unsure about what to wear, call and ask the host or someone who knows the dress code or the proper attire. When in doubt, dress conservatively. For work, take cues from senior employees or your supervisor. It is always better to be a little overdressed than underdressed.

- Dress how you want to be perceived. In the workplace, those who dress professionally may be more likely to catch the attention of upper management

1

and to be seen as candidates for better positions.

- Dress for your shape, your personality, and your needs. Develop a consistent style that takes into account your size and shape. Avoid attire that makes you feel uncomfortable. You don't have to have expensive clothes to create a good look for you.

- Update your clothes regularly. If you still look like you did ten years ago, it's time for a makeover. Get rid of clothes you haven't worn within at least the last eighteen months or for the past two seasons. Chances are you will not wear those clothes again. Give them away or try selling them at a resale or consignment store. Then with the money you receive, buy new items.

- Don't worry about trends. They come and go quickly, and you won't get your money's worth for that garment you just had to have. Besides, not everyone looks good in trendy fashions.

- Go for quality over quantity. A few well-made items will last a lot longer than less expensive clothes.

- Shoes are critical. Again, a few well-made shoes will work with your professional and personal wardrobe. Always keep them clean, shined, and well heeled.

- Don't wait until the last minute to plan your wardrobe choices. You'll start the day feeling better if you haven't hurried deciding what to wear in the morning. Put your clothes out the night before with all accessories. You may change your mind in the morning, but at least you have a starting point.

- Take your time shopping. If you need something for a special occasion, shop for it in advance. Don't shop under pressure. If you shop at the last moment, you may not be pleased with your selection, and your appearance may not send the right message. You may also end up spending more money because you have to buy what is available.
- Make sure your clothes are never stained, wrinkled, or missing buttons. Runs in nylons or slight holes are unacceptable. These things detract from your best overall look.
- Never forget the importance of good grooming to your overall appearance. Your hair, nails, makeup, and personal hygiene should always be top on your list.
- Attention to detail is the key. Accessories can dress up an outfit and help you express your personality. Just be careful not to overdo it. Simple can be beautiful.
- Always check your appearance from all angles in a full-length mirror before leaving home (and when exiting a restroom).

Necessities

- A jacket or sweater
- A pair of good quality shoes
- One piece of nice jewelry (not necessarily expensive but fashionable and appropriate)
- A quality watch
- A wallet, handbag, or briefcase

- Lint brush (Keep one at home, in your desk and in your travel bag.)
- Sewing kit (travel bag also)
- Iron and ironing board
- Full-length mirror
- Shoe polish (Also have a polish sponge for travel.)

Makeup

- You are going to work, not appearing on stage. Don't overdo your makeup for the office. Keep it light during the day. A moisturizer and foundation are a good start. A little powder, blush, eyeliner, mascara, and lipstick should be enough.
- Select blends and colors that bring out your highlights and compliment your skin color.
- Remember to allow enough time each morning to apply makeup. Don't apply it in your car as you are arriving in the parking lot or, even worse, put it on at your desk.

Hair

- Your hairstyle should be appropriate for your facial shape, hair type, personality, profession and lifestyle. It should be complimentary to you and easy to take care of. Consulting a stylist might be beneficial.
- Do not come to work with your hair partially dry or style your hair at your desk.

- Consider your hairstyle periodically. Is the style too young-looking for your age, or does it make you look too old?
- The condition of your hair is also important for your overall professional look. Keep it trimmed and styled.
- Women, watch what you wear in your hair, including scrunchies and clips. Those may be great for the weekend or a hike in the mountains but not for your office appearance. Choose hair accessories that lend a polished look.
- For men, gray hair is distinguished. Gray hair on women shouts aging, but you have options. A stylish cut can flatter silver or graying hair. It is best to consult a stylist before you decide to test hair colors on your own hair.
- Dandruff is common. If you have it use special shampoos and treatments.

Handbags/Briefcases

- Your handbag or purse should suit you. Make sure that your handbag is not too large and inappropriate for your size.
- You do not need to carry everything you own in your purse. Leave some personal items in your desk drawer.
- The handbag should be durable and coordinated with your clothes and your style.
- One work handbag is appropriate, so you don't have to change purses every day.
- A briefcase on wheels is ideal for travel.

Feet and Shoes

- Is an open-toed sandal that you would wear to the beach appropriate for work? I don't think so. Even with some offices in the business casual mode, that is still too casual. Watch what you put on your feet.
- Men should wear socks to work. Even if you have on a shirt and slacks, wearing no socks takes your outfit about ten steps lower. A nylon sock would be more appropriate.
- All shoes should be good quality, shined and in good condition. Shoes should not be scuffed and the heels should not be worn down.
- If women are able to wear a dressy sandal, then nylons need not be worn. But should you go bare-legged? If so, then do it tastefully. Have your skirt at an appropriate length, and make sure your sandals are dressy and correct for the workplace. If your legs are extremely pale, have veins, or are on the heavier side, opt for hosiery and forget the sandals.
- If you do go for the open-toed sandal look, then make sure your toes are ready for display. They must be manicured and polished. No matter how pretty the sandal, some toes should not be exposed to the public.
- If you do wear sandals, 99 percent of the time you should not have socks on. I am still searching for that 1 percent when you should!

Bare Arms

- Bare arms are considered very casual, and in most offices arms should be covered.
- If you wear a sleeveless blouse or sweater/shell, tie a cardigan sweater over your shoulders or cover up with a jacket or sweater.

A Few Hints

- Beware of fads and fashion trends. If they don't fit your lifestyle or your body style, save your money for more suitable outfits that will endure more than one season.
- Do not wear clothes that are too tight or too short. You will look heavier and shorter.
- Fingernails should be manicured and polished. Long dark-colored nails with designs are not appropriate for the office.
- Men should not wear short socks that reveal leg when they sit down. Socks don't have to be up to the knee but should be long enough to cover the leg when sitting.
- Ties for men have become bolder and more expressive, but be sure your office or meetings are ready for this creativity. If not, a classic tie will always work. Make sure your tie is long enough. It should reach the belt, with the narrow end even with or a little bit shorter than the wide end. Tall or large men should buy extra-long ties.

- Remember, men, when you sit down to eat, the tie remains in the center of your body. Do not flip it over your shoulder or tuck it into your shirt. This would not create a good first impression.
- A man should be well groomed, with any facial hair neatly trimmed.

THE POINT IS . . .
A professional appearance impresses others, boosts your self-confidence, and ensures you are ready for any business opportunity.

TWO

Mastering Communication Technology

●　●　●　●　●　●　●　●

Computerized office environments, telecommuting, and all the electronic innovations of the past two decades have created a new set of situations to challenge professional behavior. I call this area "netiquette," but it includes much more than the Internet. As handy as some electronic tools can be, they also create irritation and interruptions. A business professional should know how to balance well-mannered attention to a client against a ringing cell phone. Shame on you if you don't!

E-mail

- E-mail is still a business communication. Watch grammar, spelling, and abbreviations. People will judge your e-mail just as critically as they judge a business letter.
- Use the subject line. It may get your message read a little faster, and the reader will be able to find the message for future referral.
- All lowercasing or all caps is difficult to read. Using all capital letters is considered the equivalent of shouting.

All lowercase is not whispering, but it is annoying.

- Don't use e-mail when a handwritten note is more appropriate.
- If you get a request addressed to numerous people, respond only to the sender unless requested to do otherwise.
- Read all your e-mail before responding. Go to the most recent ones first. You may discover earlier messages have been amended or updated.
- Be careful with your password. Protect it.
- Be discreet about sending jokes and other questionable comments. You never know who may receive or pass on something you thought would remain private.
- Respond to e-mail.
- Ask to be removed from unwanted routing lists.
- Some companies can and will monitor employee e-mail. Legally, employers have the right to read all employee e-mail on their computer systems. In some companies, e-mail can be grounds for termination.
- You can sometimes stop e-mail after it has been sent (if done before the recipient reads it), but even if you delete your e-mail, it does not go away forever. It can be recovered and traced.
- Don't let e-mail (or any other written form of communication) substitute for discussing important issues in person.
- If e-mailing internationally, keep the language as formal as possible. Casual language, clichés, jargon, and slang words or phrases may have different meanings elsewhere.

- Make sure you have a "signature line" at the end of your e-mail message. Quick reference to your full name, title, company, phone, fax, e-mail address, and Web site will make it easy for people to contact you.
- If you are out of your office for an extended time, use the "Out of Office" message so people sending you e-mail will know that you are not available to answer immediately. You can also provide information about your return, another way to contact you if necessary, and any other details, but keep your message short and concise.

Cell Phones

- Turn cell phones off in meetings, restaurants, movies and churches. Turn to vibrating signal for a call you can't miss.
- Advise other participants before a meeting starts that you are expecting a call you must handle immediately. When the call comes in (vibrating signal), excuse yourself and handle it quickly.
- Use your cell phone discreetly on airplanes. They are not allowed while in flight. Talk softly to avoid disturbing others.
- If you must make a phone call in a busy place, walk to a less crowded area.
- If you must use your cell phone in the car, always pull over and stop to make or receive a call, or purchase hands-free accessories so you do not have to take your

hands off the wheel. (In some states, it is now illegal to use cell phones while driving.) Remember the other people on the road while you are using your cell phone.

- If you place a call and are disconnected, it is your responsibility to call the person back immediately.
- Avoid borrowing someone's cell phone, but if you must, keep the call brief.
- Cell phones really do bother other people, so keep your voice at a lower level. People around you do not want to hear your conversations.

Phones

- Answer properly with your name and company name or proper greeting for your company or business. Don't anticipate someone to be calling. Always treat the phone call as if it could be your boss or the chairman of the board on the line.
- Announce your full name when you answer. Speak clearly and slowly.
- Give the person on the line your undivided attention. Avoid eating, drinking, typing, or sending faxes while using the phone.
- Change your voice mail when you are traveling, in meetings, or will be out of the office for an extended period. Leave a number where you can be reached if possible.
- Leave exact messages on a voice mail to those you call (why are you calling, what you need/want, and a

good time to call you back). Leave your full name, company name and title, and the time and day you are calling. Say your phone number clearly and slowly— two times—in the beginning and at the end of the conversation. Leave your phone number even if you call the person regularly. He may not have your number handy.

- Follow through on all phone requests as soon as possible.
- Be conscious of the time, particularly with international communications or when calling virtual/home offices.

Speaker Phones/Conference Calls

- Be cautious of the use of a speaker phone. Some people do not like being on a speaker.
- Do not answer a call on the speaker phone. Once on a call if you need to switch to the speaker phone, explain why, and ask if the person would mind.
- Your business conversations should be one-on-one and not broadcast throughout the office. Use your speaker phone discreetly.
- Identify everyone in the room who will be participating in the call.
- When you speak, move closer to the phone, and make sure only one person is speaking at a time.
- Identify yourself when beginning to speak if others are not familiar with you or your voice.
- Do not have side conversations during your call. They can be very disrupting and make it difficult to hear.

- Indicate to your listeners if you have to leave during the call and if you will be returning.

Voice Mail/Answering Machines

- State the facts briefly, but be sure to provide enough information. Don't leave a message that rambles or gives numerous instructions.
- Include your first and last name, company name, and your title (if the person you are calling is not familiar with you). Don't assume everyone will know or remember you.
- Give the reason for your call and your full telephone number. Speak slowly and clearly and repeat the number.
- Never leave an important message, such as a change of a meeting time or location, without following up to confirm it was received.
- Never leave vague, mysterious, or teasing messages. They could be misinterpreted and lead to embarrassment or the wrong impression. You want to convey professionalism in all business dealings.
- Don't call back repeatedly to leave the same message if the person has not returned your call.
- In your office, don't choose an answering system that allows people to leave only very short messages. It is annoying and expensive to have to make repeated calls to an answering machine.
- Leave a businesslike greeting on your line. Be enthu-

siastic, but avoid jokes, weird music, or cute sayings.

- On your machine, ask those calling to leave their name, company, response number, the time they called, and a brief message.
- Provide callers with information about when you will return to the office, a back-up person or number to call, and any other brief information deemed necessary.
- Smile when you are leaving the greeting on your own voice mail machine. It makes your tone friendlier.

Fax and Copy Machines

- Be courteous. Don't monopolize printers, copiers, or fax machines.
- Sending an unsolicited twenty-page document may tie up the receiver's fax line. Ask clients if they would prefer to have a long document mailed.
- Don't forward junk faxes, jokes, personal, or sensitive information by fax. Other people could see it before it reaches the recipient.
- Faxes are not appropriate for all communications. Write your personal notes, invitations, thank-you notes, congratulations, or condolences on good stationery or printed cards.
- Be conscious of the hour of the night or morning that a fax is sent, especially when dealing with international communications or virtual/home offices.
- Always include a fax cover sheet that includes your full name, fax number, phone number, and address.

Make it easy for the recipient to respond to you. Also include the number of pages being sent, including the cover sheet.

Laptops/Notebooks

- Be careful when traveling with a laptop. It is tempting for thieves.
- Because of security issues, you must send your laptop through the security gate on the conveyor belt rather than carrying it through the metal detector.
- If you use your laptop in flight, consider the people beside and in front of you. If they want to sleep and you are constantly clicking the keys, that constant noise can be extremely annoying.

THE POINT IS . . .
Remember, a handwritten note is still the first choice in communicating a personal message.

THREE

Behaving Professionally in the Workplace

●●●●●●●

Your office behavior affects how seriously you are taken by your supervisor and can affect your progress within your department and the organization. These brief thoughts about office behavior are good advice for someone beginning a career, but it is never too late to start acting more professionally. Review these points and resolve to correct any bad habits you may have acquired.

Personal Matters

- In the morning, start work at the designated time. This does not mean after a 15-minute breakfast in the break room or at your desk. Eat breakfast at home or come in a few minutes early if you need to have your meal in the office kitchen or break room.
- Because labor laws require breaks throughout the workday, it is best to leave your work area for breaks and lunch. If you are asked to work through lunch, exceptions can be made on specific occasions.
- As much as possible, avoid initiating or receiving personal phone calls or e-mail on company time. If you

receive a personal call, give it three to five minutes. Then tell the caller you have to get back to work and offer to return the call during lunch or your break or after work hours.

- Do not create or repeat office gossip, whether it concerns business or personal matters.

Work Responsibilities

- When you are given a responsibility, assume charge of the task. If it appears that time will not allow you to handle or complete the job, advise your supervisor of the situation as soon as you realize it and request more time or negotiate an acceptable solution.

- Give updates and status reports to your supervisor when you are working on a project. Don't wait for your supervisor to follow up. Don't let the supervisor assume you understand the job or think the job is being handled if you are encountering difficulties.

- If you make a mistake, take responsibility, admit the problem, and then move on. Don't pass the buck or make excuses.

- Never say, "It is not my job," or "It is not my responsibility." As a member of a team, you should share responsibilities. Admit when you don't know an answer, but search for solutions and then respond. Make it your job. And respond quickly.

More Hints for the Office

- Remember that a client could phone or come into the office at any time. Be aware that your behavior or conversations may be subject to scrutiny by clients as well as by your supervisor/employer.
- Minimal or no alcoholic beverages should be consumed during a luncheon, and minimal consumption is wise during an evening function. Exceeding the legal limit for alcohol is grounds for dismissal from most companies. Remember, when you attend a business function, you represent your company and should always follow company policies.
- If food is brought or sent to your office by a supplier, vendor, or customer, share it. Take a portion and then place it where all members of the company may enjoy it. If a gift comes to a specific department, it is still good to share with other staff. If food remains at the end of the day, it can be taken home.
- Be a positive problem-solver. If you detect an operations problem, don't point it out without offering a few suggestions for a solution.

THE POINT IS . . .
True professionals take responsibility
and act responsibly.

FOUR

Networking: How to Work a Room

●●●●●●●●

Receptions, association luncheons, and other networking events are occasions to meet new people and make contacts that may lead to potential clients. But if you spend the time with friends, focus on the buffet or bar, and leave without accomplishing some business goals, you've failed to take advantage of great opportunities. The solution is to set goals before you enter the room—meet people, exchange business cards, and perhaps pave the way for future contacts or meetings. It is not appropriate to use receptions or networking events to present a proposal or contract or to conduct a business meeting.

Attitude

For some people, entering a room full of strangers is easy, but for others it is pure torture. Your attitude plays a major role when you attend a reception or any business function. You can enter a room with any of the following attitudes:

- There is nobody interesting to talk to here.
- I'd rather be in my hotel room watching television.

- I'm here to party, not to network.
- I am shy, fear meeting strangers, feel uncomfortable and awkward, and lack self-confidence.
- I'm here to meet as many people as I can, and I hope to find some future business.

Both introverts and extroverts attend business and social gatherings. You need to find the group that fits you best. But your ultimate goal is to mix with all groups.

The Basic Steps

- Enter the room with your head held high, and tell yourself you can do it.
- Look for two or three people together and approach them.
- Start with a solid handshake.
- Look each person straight in the eyes as you introduce yourself.
- Listen carefully to their names. Repeat their names, and then try to use them again during your conversation. Repeating the names will help you remember them, but try not to be too obvious.
- Turn your body toward the person you are meeting. Do not be distracted or look all around the room for other people to meet. Give your undivided attention to the person speaking. Be attentive and listen to what that person is saying.
- Exchange business cards. If someone has a special

request, write it on the card so you can respond quickly. Just be sure to ask the person if it is okay to write on their card. Do not leave anything to memory. After meeting numerous people for the first time, it becomes very difficult to remember what they have requested.

- Eventually, excuse yourself, and move on to other people. (See tips below.)

Conversation Tips

- A little chitchat is good in the beginning. Easy topics include names, hometown, and work. Perhaps you'll find a commonality.
- Avoid controversial topics.
- Pick up cues from name badges if people are wearing them.
- Be proactive; initiate conversation rather than waiting. Ask open-ended questions, such as "I see you are from XYZ Company. What do you do for them?"
- Include everyone in your conversation.
- Stick to familiar topics to help you feel at ease.
- Respond to comments and questions of others.
- Allow others to talk. Don't monopolize the conversation.
- Gossip is verboten. Don't talk about people.
- Expressing opinions is fine but don't get on a soapbox, teach, preach, or attempt to impress (name dropping).
- If the other person is obviously bored or not responding, end the conversation.
- Remember to listen attentively.

How to Move On

- Since the goal should be to work the room, avoid getting trapped in one conversation all evening.
- Thank the others for the conversation, express pleasure in meeting them, or use another appropriate transition to depart.
- You may mention getting something to eat or drink or needing to find another person before the event ends.
- Take them to meet another person and then you can gracefully move on.
- Always start and end your conversation with a handshake.
- Excuse yourself graciously and promise to respond or to anticipate a response if future contact was requested or promised.

Making the Most of Networking Receptions

- If a reception is held in your own company, where you know a lot of the employees, you should meet people outside your department whom you may just pass in the hallway. If a seated dinner follows the reception, sit at a different department's table.
- The reception may be during an industry convention or meeting. Circulate out of your security area and meet new people. Don't stay with coworkers and friends. Set a goal of how many new people you will meet that evening. Make it a fun adventure.
- If the reception occurs during your first time at a

group meeting, at a new church or at a new venue, make the most of it. Go into the reception with a great attitude and meet as many people as you can.

- Be an active participant. Don't hide. Don't go to a corner of a room and simply observe.
- It is difficult to shake hands and meet someone when you have a plate in one hand and a drink in the other. Mingle, work the room and then get something to eat and drink. Don't go immediately to the food area and put a plate in your hand, and don't go to the bar area and hang out there all evening.

Pre-event Planning

- Do your homework. Find out who is attending and what you may need to know when you meet these people.
- Review the attendee list before going to the reception. The list may be a part of your registration packet at the convention, or you may need to call the company and request a list.
- Be organized. Go prepared with business cards. Keep them where they can be reached easily to present to your new contacts. A good hint is to wear a jacket with pockets. Keep your cards in the right pocket, and put contacts' cards in the left.
- Know why you are there. Are you looking for business or trying to meet specific people? Are you networking or trying to increase your visibility? Are you going in

place of your boss to represent your company or just taking advantage of the free food and drink?

- If it is a reception and a trade show, you can send out advance mailings such as post cards, flyers, notes, or letters to all attendees in time to reach them before the show. Let them know a little about your company, where your booth will be, and your promotions. A prize or drawing usually will bring more people to your booth.

- If the function is for a smaller group of people, call contacts prior to the networking opportunity and see if they can meet you there. Ask for a specific short period of time, instead of taking their time during the entire reception or trade show.

- Remember, a reception is a time to exchange cards and set up future meetings, not to conduct business. But at a trade show, you can discuss business and maybe even close a deal.

Tips for Trade Show Exhibitors

- Before the trade show, send out mailers with your booth number (if available) and information about your give-aways or games. Make sure attendees receive your mailer in plenty of time to schedule your booth into their plans.

- Try to get a good location for your booth. Or try to get a position next to a popular location or the food area.

- Make your booth area approachable. Don't stand behind a table or sit in a chair.

- Many exhibitors now dress in golf shirts with company logos or similar outfits, depending on their product or market. Casual clothes and comfortable shoes are great for the long hours spent on trade show floors.
- Greet everyone, and invite them into your booth area.
- Have give-aways, games, or gimmicks.
- Know the difference between a prospect, someone just browsing, and someone stopping for your gift or food.
- Respond immediately to any requests made by possible clients.

Tips for Trade Show Attendees

- Do your homework, and be prepared when you enter the trade show floor.
- Set measurable specific goals that fit your business strategies and help you stay focused and on track.
- Know whom you want to meet and plan your strategy to meet everyone within the given time of the trade show.
- Be sure to carry a good supply of business cards so you won't run out mid-way into a meeting or a trade show, and carry your cards with you at all times.
- You are there to make new contacts and business opportunities for your company, not to socialize with friends.
- Make the best use of your energies and talents by planning appointments with vendors when you are fresh and not overly tired.

- Keep files of materials gathered at trade shows so you have ready access to vendors' information.
- Follow up after the show to ensure you have all the information you need.

Follow Up

- Immediately upon returning to your office, send a handwritten note to every potential client you met. Even better, carry note cards with you and write them from the trade show or meeting site at the end of each day, but mail them from your hometown and use regular postage, not metered mail, for a more personal touch.
- Follow up any request within twenty-four to forty-eight hours. Don't let contacts' business cards stack up. Make the phone calls you need to make, and file or enter into your database the contact information you need for future use.
- It takes less than three minutes to write a thank-you note and address the envelope. Those three minutes can make a great impression on a client or potential client.
- Be careful about e-mail responses. If you are simply sending requested information, then e-mail is appropriate, but never send an e-mail in place of a handwritten thank-you note.
- Be as good as your word. If you promised to send something, research something, or do something for a client, then do it! And do it as soon as possible.

- Does the person's request need a phone call? If so, do your research, and respond quickly. Should you leave a voice mail if the client is not available? Yes, but tell the client a good time to reach you or when you will try again.
- Your Web site can be a starting point for clients. Print your Web address on your business cards.

THE POINT IS . . .
Networking can create business opportunities.
Meet people, listen, and follow up.

FIVE

Dining and Table Et

● ● ● ● ● ● ● ●

Granted, growing up in a fast-food world does not provide many opportunities for learning the finer points of dining etiquette. But in a business setting, minding your manners can make a lasting impression. The tips in this chapter provide the basics about what you should and should not do in a business/formal setting. The following chapters will help you negotiate a complex table setting, give advice about hosting a business dinner, and being on your best behavior at other meal functions.

Setting the Table

Simple dinner meals
- Knives and spoons are on the right.
- Forks and napkins are on the left (except for the cocktail fork that is on the far right).
- Glassware/crystal is on the right.
- Coffee cup and saucer are on the right or are placed before or during dessert.
- Plates, such as a salad plate or bread-and-butter plate, are on the left.

laborate dining

- Usually replace the flatware and china before each course.
- Dessert utensils are placed horizontally above the dinner plate. The dessert spoon (bowl facing left) goes above the fork (tines facing right).

Styles of Eating

AMERICAN: An inefficient style of eating/dining but common in the United States. In a formal setting, cut one bite at a time; at other times, cut two or three pieces at the most.

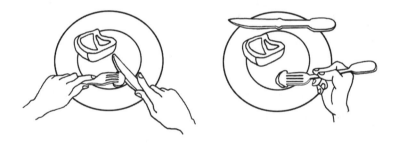

CONTINENTAL/EUROPEAN: The knife remains in the right hand and the fork in the left. Only one bite is cut at a time.

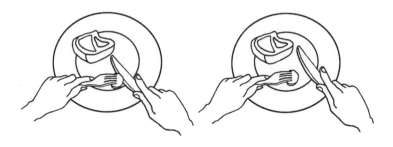

Dining Rules to Live By

1. SILVERWARE: The rule to remember is once you pick up any piece of your silverware, it never touches the table again. Don't let your silverware rest partially on the table and partially on your plate. In most cases, work from the outside in with your silverware.

2. THE "B" AND "D" RULE OR BMW: To get your bearings when you are seated, think BMW—bread, meal, water. Your bread, meal and water go left to right, just like the letters. Some people remember "b" for bread and "d" for drink. Note that the lower case letter "b" on your left hand facing the plate stands for bread and the lower case "d" on your right hand facing the plate stands for drink.

3. HOSTS: Take your cues from them. This includes where to sit, when to place your napkin on your lap, when to start the meal, make toasts, and/or discuss business. Keep pace with the hosts while they are eating (you may need to slow down or speed up). Finish the meal and place your napkin on the table to the left of your plate when they do or when you are finished.

4. WHEN TO START TO EAT: Wait until everyone is served. If there are hosts, they either will start to eat or will make a gesture or comment for guests to enjoy the

meal. When the host begins, you may also start. If a person at your table has requested a special meal, he should instruct everyone else at the table to begin since his meal may be delayed. Feel free to begin your meal.

5. NAPKIN: Place the napkin on your lap as soon as you are seated. Your napkin is not a flag to signal the start of a race, so don't flap it all around. Just place the unfolded napkin on your lap. If it is large, leave it only half open. If your silverware is rolled into the napkin on the table at your setting, just take the entire napkin and place it on your lap and unroll it. Then place the silverware on the table in the correct positions. If you leave the table, place your napkin on the chair and gently push the chair back under the table. At the end of the meal, pick up the napkin from your lap and loosely place it on the table to the left of your plate, not on the plate. Never use the napkin as a hanky or tissue. If you sneeze, you can blot, but don't blow your nose or rub your face. Don't wipe your mouth with one hand while holding a knife or fork with the other.

6. DROPPING SOMETHING OR USING THE WRONG ITEM: If you drop a piece of your silverware or your napkin, let it go. You can either ask for another one or the wait staff will notice and replace it for you. If your neighbor happens to take your napkin or maybe your bread-and-butter plate or starts drinking your coffee,

let it go. You can place your bread on your entrée plate or ask the waiter for another glass, napkin, or silverware. Try to do all of this without drawing attention to your neighbor. Don't panic if you use the wrong piece of flatware. Just keep using it and ask the waiter for a replacement when you need it.

7. DOUBLE-DIPPING: It is unsanitary to dip a chip or hors d'oeuvre into a sauce/dip—take a bite—and then dip it again. Either break the piece of food in half so you can dip both pieces or dip only the initial piece. If possible, place some of the dip on your own plate. Then you don't have to worry about double-dipping.

8. BREAD: First place the butter on your plate. Do not go directly to the bread with the butter. Break off only one bite-sized piece at a time from the slice of bread or roll. Butter that piece, set the knife down on the plate, and then eat that one piece. Do not butter the whole roll or slice of bread (or even half) and then just start to bite off pieces.

9. SALT AND PEPPER: Remember the salt and pepper are a pair. They go together. Even if someone asks you to pass just the salt, pick up both the salt and pepper and pass them together. Place them on the table next to the person and they can select what they wish. Do not hand them to the person making the request. When setting the table, put salt and pepper together at both ends of the table.

10. THE SQUIRTING LEMON: Cup the lemon before you squeeze it into a drink or over your fish or meal. After you have squeezed the lemon, place it on the side of your plate or drop it into the drink. If the lemon is covered in a mesh, then set it to the side of your plate.

11. SWEETENER PACKETS: Do not shake or flick packets. Place the empty packages under your iced tea plate, coffee saucer or entrée plate. A good wait staff will see them and take them away when they clear your plates. Other items like wrappers from crackers and straws or plastic creamer cups can be handled the same way, or just place them on the edge of your saucer or bread plate.

12. LIPSTICK AND MAKEUP: Don't apply makeup at the table. If you absolutely must, take the lipstick and apply it without lip liner, the use of a mirror, or calling attention to yourself. A better alternative is to excuse yourself and go to the restroom to apply any lipstick or touch up.

Minding Your Table Manners

• When you approach the table, enter your chair from the left. Purses, briefcases, and all personal articles should stay off the table. Put them on the floor to your right or under your seat. If it is not a part of the meal or table setting, it should not be on the table during the meal. When you leave the table, exit to your right, and pick up your belongings.

- Never chew with your mouth open, and no matter how urgent you think it is to talk, don't do it with your mouth full. Wait gracefully, swallow, then speak.
- Always remember to sit up straight. You don't need to be at a 90-degree angle but also don't be at a 45-degree angle to your plate. Lean forward slightly to eat and then back again.
- Keep your elbows off the table. If you're in doubt about your hands, put them in your lap. Whether you are right- or left-handed, your arms and elbows should always stay close to you.
- Burping is so embarrassing, but if it happens, cover your mouth and just say, "Excuse me."
- Never pick your teeth at the table. If you have something in your teeth take a drink of water, and if that doesn't work excuse yourself and go to the restroom.
- Don't ask questions. If someone at your table takes a pill, don't ask if they are sick or why they are taking it. If someone gets up to leave the table for whatever reason, again, make no comments.
- Watch your speed. Keep pace with everyone at your table. Remember the rule about following the pace of the host.
- When you have completed your meal, leave your plate in front of you, don't push it away or move it. Don't be so relaxed that you tilt or push your chair back.
- Respect fellow diners. Even if you are seated in a restaurant's smoking section, always ask permission to

smoke. Do not start to smoke while others are still eating, and never use your plate as an ashtray.

- Try to postpone business discussions until the end of the meal if time will permit. Do not spread your papers over the table. A portfolio works best to keep everything organized and confined. If time is an issue, place your order and then begin your business meeting. Respect the time of your client when conducting a meal meeting.

Some Hints about Food

- Always pass food to the right (also with business card exchanges).
- If your soup, coffee, or any hot item has steam coming off the top, give it a few seconds to cool down. Don't blow on your food or drink.
- Don't salt or season your food before you taste it.
- Cut one bite of meat or food at a time in formal settings. In a less formal setting, you can cut two or three pieces at the most, but it is a good habit to stick with one.
- Refrain from dunking anything in your soup, milk, or coffee. Cookies, donuts, or crackers should not be crumbled or dunked. Treat crackers like bread and break off one piece at a time, butter and eat.
- Items with handles should be passed with the handle toward the other person. It helps them accept the bowl or pitcher. If an item is too hot, set it next to the person or if the platter is heavy, you can offer to help

hold it while they take their food off the platter. Then they can assist the person to their right.

- If a long-handled teaspoon is provided for iced tea, use it only to stir sugar or sweetener into the tea. If a small plate is provided with your iced tea, then place the spoon on this small plate. If there is not a plate under your glass, then use your dinner plate. If no teaspoon is provided, use the other spoon at your place setting.

- If the entrée and the salad are served together, you may use the entrée fork for both. You don't have to keep switching back and forth between the two forks. Also, if a salad is the main course, then you can use the entrée fork. Again, it is pretty safe to start from the outside and work your way in with silverware.

- When in doubt, eat with a utensil rather than with your fingers, even those foods that you may eat with your hands at home. Use a fork to cut French fries into bite-sized pieces unless they are served with a hamburger or sandwich, and then you can use your fingers. Eat bacon with a fork unless it is too crisp, then fingers are acceptable, too. Chicken, or any other meat at a business meal, is not finger food. You should use the knife and fork.

- If you don't know how to eat something that comes with your meal, leave it, or watch to see how others eat it and follow their lead.

- If it's on your plate, it's meant to be eaten. So enjoy!

Soup Guidelines

- Lean forward slightly to eat the soup.
- Dip the spoon sideways into the soup, going away from you.
- Just skim the top of the soup, don't fill the spoon completely.
- Sip off the edge, not from the front of your spoon. Don't put the whole spoon in your mouth.
- If you need that last spoonful, tilt the soup bowl away from you.
- If soup is served in a cup with one or two handles, you may pick up the soup cup and drink it. If there are two handles, hold both handles.
- Do not crumble crackers into your soup. Treat crackers like bread, one bite at a time. Rest the crackers on the dish under the soup plate.
- You may put several oyster crackers in the soup at a time. Leave the extra crackers on the dish under the soup plate.
- Don't blow on the soup. Let it cool and then eat.
- Both soup cups and soup plates should be served with saucers or plates beneath them. When your soup is served in a soup cup, the spoon should lie on the saucer when not in use or when you have completed the soup. But when soup is served in a soup plate, the spoon is left in the soup plate instead of on the dish under it.

Wait Staff Interactions

- Wait staff are trained so let them do their job. Allow them to take your plate and clear the table. Don't stack your plates or hand them to the wait staff. An exception: If you are seated in a far corner or awkward place, then it may be appropriate to hand your plate to the waiter.
- Be considerate of waiters when they are serving a large setting for a convention or meal. Allow them to set all the meals before you make any special requests like extra dressing, another drink, or hot tea instead of coffee.
- Courses are normally set from the left and removed from the right. An easy way to remember is "remove" from "right." All drinks are served and removed from the right. It helps to know which direction to lean while the wait staff places or removes your dishes.
- If you need to get a waiter's attention, just raise your hand quietly. You do not need to get everyone's attention in the entire room by waving your hand frantically, signaling with your napkin, or raising your voice.
- Remember: It takes only a second to turn to your waiter and say "thank you."

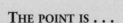

THE POINT IS . . .

Don't be bound by rules of behavior. If the client or host picks up the chicken or lamp chop with his or her fingers, feel free to do so, too. Consideration of others and forgetfulness of oneself are of paramount importance in the host/client relationship.

SIX

Negotiating the Tabletop

● ● ● ● ● ● ●

Your first encounter with multiple utensils and glasses does not have to be intimidating. Formal table settings are laid out logically. You need to remember only a few simple rules to be able to read the tabletop road map. This chapter gives course-by-course directions to get you to the end of the meal without a breakdown in your good manners.

Utensils

- There can be as many as three forks to the left of the service plate and three knives to the right. You should never find more than three of one utensil at a place setting.

- The only exceptions will be the butter knife that is placed on the bread plate and a fourth fork, the small oyster fork, which is placed at the extreme right of the place setting and is used for oysters or shrimp cocktail. Its tines should be resting in the bowl of the soup spoon.

- After the soup spoon, and working from outside to inside on both sides, are the fish fork and fish knife, followed by the meat fork and knife. Next to the dinner plate are the salad fork and knife, unless the salad is served first, in which case, it is farthest away from the plate. (See illustration on next page.)

- The simple rule about cutlery use: Always start from the outside and work your way in, course by course, toward the center.

Glasses

- Glasses follow the same progression as the silverware, moving from right to left, from the outside to the center.

- The sherry glass is positioned above the soup spoon (sherry being served to accompany soup); the white wine glass (smaller bowl than the red wine glass) is above the fish knife and the red wine glass (often served with meat) is located above the meat knife. Behind the red wine glass is the water goblet, the largest glass. The champagne flute (to accompany dessert) is to the right of the water goblet. If only a water glass is placed on the table, it would be at the tip of the knife.

- If the wine is cold, hold the glass by the stem. Sip from the glass and never wave it. If you are drinking red wine, it is acceptable to hold the glass by the bowl and stem, since the heat from your hand will not affect the taste of the wine. Left-handed people should remember to use the right hand to drink wine or water so it can be replaced correctly on the right hand side.

- The sherry glass is removed from the place setting when the soup plates are cleared. All the other glasses—the water goblet and the red and white wine glasses—remain on the table. You may ask to have your wine glasses removed if you will not be drinking wine.

First Course

- The oyster fork is used to eat clams, oysters, and shrimp cocktail. Because shrimp cocktail is frequently served in a pedestal dish, it would be difficult to cut the shrimp with a knife without toppling the dish. Just eat it from the fork by taking several small bites. If shrimp is served on a flat plate, you may use your knife to cut it. The lettuce in the dish is not to be eaten. It is for decoration only.
- The wait staff will remove this course from the right then place your soup plate and saucer from the left.

Soup Course

- You will find your soup spoon on the right. Lean forward slightly to eat your soup, dip the spoon sideways into the soup at the edge nearest you. Just skim the surface of the soup and move the spoon away from you.
- Sip silently from the side of the spoon without making any noise. Don't put the entire spoon in your mouth. If you must have that last little bit, tip the bowl away from you and continue to spoon the soup from the outer edge of the bowl.
- If the soup is served in a cup with handles on both sides, it is perfectly appropriate to pick up the cup by both handles and sip the soup.

- If you are served crackers with your soup course, put the soup spoon down and take a bite of the cracker. (Remember, if soup is served in a cup, the spoon rests on the plate beneath, but if soup is served in a larger bowl, the spoon stays in the bowl.) Do not hold the cracker in one hand, the soup spoon in the other, and alternate between them. Don't break crackers into your soup. Use the same procedure as for bread. Break off the bite that you will eat and then place the remaining cracker on the under plate. If oyster crackers are served, place them on your under plate and add a few at a time to your soup.

Bread and Butter

- Usually there are no bread-and-butter plates at a formal dinner, but this is one practice that may be evolving. If there are no bread plates, do not ask for them.
- In other meals, the bread-and-butter plate will be to your left. A separate butter knife may be resting on the plate. If there is no butter knife, it is appropriate to use your dinner knife to butter your bread or roll. Leave the knife on the bread plate until the main course is served; then move it to the entrée plate.
- In very casual settings you may find only a bread basket on the table with a shared butter dish. Offer the basket to your guests before serving yourself. (Pass to the right.) Use your clean fork to place a pat of butter on your dinner plate and put your bread or roll on the plate.

- Remember the rule to always break bread, never cut it. Then butter only a small piece that you will eat at that time. Do the same with rolls. It is inappropriate to sit at the table with half a buttered roll in your hand, taking bites as you are talking to other people at the table.

Fish Course

- For your fish course you will probably have a fish knife. It has a distinctive sword-like shape.
- Hold the fish knife like a pencil so you can use the broad side of the blade to lift and separate sections of the fish.
- If you are served a boneless fillet, you will not need to use the fish knife. Leave it on the table and cut the fillet with the side of the fish fork. This fork is on your extreme left and resembles a salad fork except the tines are wider. If you would like, you can use your

knife to push the food if you are eating in the Continental or European style.

Salad

- Salads can be served before the entrée or after it and immediately before dessert. The cutlery will be placed according to the timing of this course. You may use your knife to cut a lettuce leaf to bite size.
- If not set in front of you as a separate course, the salad plate will be on your left, above or beside the bread-and-butter plate. If the entrée and salad are served at the same time, you may use the entrée fork for both.
- When the main courses are finished, a waiter will clear the table, removing the salt and pepper shakers and sweeping away crumbs. The glasses will remain. Remember not to stack your plates or to hand your plate(s) to the wait staff. Allow them to handle the removal.

Dessert

- In formal dining, the waiter will bring the dessert plate, upon which will be the finger bowl on its doily, with the dessert fork and spoon.
- Place the silverware on the table on either side of the plate. Lightly dip your fingertips into the bowl and pat gently on the towel provided or on your napkin. Then move the bowl and doily to the upper left of your plate.
- If using European or Continental style, you can eat

with the spoon and use the fork as the pusher. If eating American style, you may use whichever piece of silverware you prefer and leave the other on the table.

- If fruits are served, they are quartered first with a sharp fruit knife and then peeled. Move discarded peel and any seeds to the side of your plate. Then cut the fruit into bite-sized pieces, which you eat with the fruit fork or, in an informal setting, with your fingers.

Finger Bowls

- Dip only the tips of your fingers into the finger bowl. Dry them on the napkin or a towel if provided. You may touch the tips of your moistened fingers to your lips and then lightly touch your napkin to your lips.
- At a dinner party in someone's home, a small crystal bowl of cool water might be presented at the beginning of the dessert course. In this case, the finger bowl is placed on a small lace or organdy doily that rests on a dessert plate. After using the finger bowl, move it with the doily to the upper left of the place setting, near where the butter plate was or just above where the forks originally were. Your empty dessert plate is now ready for the dessert.

Inedible Items

- The simple rule is to take inedible items out of your mouth the same way they were put in. In other words, remove grape seeds with your fingers because you eat grapes with your fingers; gristle is removed with your fork; pits, such as prune pits, are removed with a spoon.

- The only exception is a fish bone. Although fish is eaten with a fork, you remove a fish bone from your mouth with your fingers. Place whatever you are removing at the edge of your plate.

Salt and Pepper

- The salt and pepper always travel together, even if someone requests only one. Place the shakers on the table in front of the person requesting them. Do not hand them to the person.
- You may encounter a little dish of salt called a salt cellar. Pass the salt cellar with the pepper shaker. The salt cellar usually has an accompanying tiny salt spoon. Use it to place a spoonful of salt at the edge of your plate and dip each forkful of food into that. If there is no spoon, use the edge of your clean knife to serve yourself a portion of salt.

Wine Selection

- Wines are changing, and the steadfast principle of white wine with fish and poultry and red wine with meat is not necessarily the rule of thumb. This little guideline may help you remember:

- CHardonnay and CHablis go well with CHicken.
- SOave is good with SOle.
- BEaujolais is a red wine to drink with BEef, as are Bordeaux and Barolo.
- Usually wines served during a meal are described as "dry," which means that they are not sweet. However, champagne is labeled differently. A champagne marked dry, or sec, is the sweetest of sparkling wines. Extra dry will be a bit less sweet. The driest champagnes are labeled brut.
- The sommelier will be happy to advise you. By all means, rely upon the wine steward's expertise and allow him to assist you in choosing appropriate wines.
- Here are some simple estimates for wine servings:
  - Three bottles of wine for a table of eight
  - Five servings per 750 ml (normal size) bottle of wine
  - Ten servings per magnum (1.5 liters) of wine

Serving Beer

In the past, beer was for picnics, night clubs, and sitting around eating pizza, but now it is much more acceptable, even in upscale restaurants. Be prepared when guests ask for beer instead of wine.

- Have attractive pilsner glasses or even fun steins (with no advertisements on them) for serving beer. Oversized red wine goblets also are acceptable. Stay away from tumblers or plastic glasses used for water or soda.

- Do not put cans or bottles of beer on the table. Pour the beer into a tall glass that will hold the entire contents of the bottle or can.
- Beer usually is served with hearty, simple food. Beer goes well with sandwiches, hamburgers, pizza, Tex-Mex food, oriental food, picnics, and barbecues. Avoid ordering beer in a fine restaurant with a delicate fish or a rich gourmet dessert.
- If you are dining with an executive who orders wine or a cocktail with the meal, it is fine for you to order beer.
- Do not walk around a reception or cocktail party carrying a bottle or can of beer. Have it poured into a tall glass.
- You may serve beer instead of wine at a business meal, but make sure the menu is informal and proper glasses are available. Always offer guests alternatives such as wine, iced tea, or coffee.

THE POINT IS . . .
Always start from the outside and work your way in, course by course, toward the center and never let your utensils touch the table after you have used them.

SEVEN

Hosting and Attending Business Meals

●●●●●●●

Hosting a well-planned business meal presents many challenges but can leave a lasting good impression on your clients. Remember, when you are participating in a business meal as either host or guest, you represent your company, and your behavior reflects on your employer as well as yourself. Although the dining table may seem more informal than the conference table, you must always demonstrate the highest professionalism and courtesy.

Seated Dinners

- If you are hosting, arrive early to finalize all plans. This includes the flow of the meal, seating arrangements, name badges, handling the bill in advance, and meeting wait staff.
- If you do not have a private room or area in the restaurant, then make sure you select an area that is a little more secluded or away from the kitchen and the main part of the facility.
- Make sure as your guests arrive that you or a staff person meets them at the door to direct them to your

seating area or reception. If it is a smaller dinner, then greet your guests at the table and introduce yourself, if necessary. Shake hands. If name badges are required, guests should receive them immediately.

- As host, you should control the luncheon/dinner. If you want specific seating, arrive early so you can place guests as they enter. If possible, use place cards for guests and place them according to rank if appropriate. (See "Table Seating" in this chapter.)

- As host, try to keep your back to the wall in order to see everyone who is coming toward you. Arrange the seating so that you have good eye contact between yourself and the most important client.

- If you are a guest, wait to sit down until you receive your host's signal. If your host sits down without signaling you where to sit, take the chair nearest you. When the waiter seats you, take the chair he offers. It usually is the best at that table.

- Enter from your left when you sit at a table and leave from the right.

- If you are introducing coworkers or clients, be specific about their names and titles and possibly even the roles they will play in the particular event, function, or project being discussed.

- Remember, no purses or other items should be placed on the table. If you have a briefcase or purse, put it to the right of your chair. You should be leaving that way and can be ready to step over it or to pick it up quickly. Be careful not to trip on the straps of a purse or briefcase, and be sure to place them out of the way of wait staff.

- Wait until the entire table is served before eating. If a person's meal is delayed for some reason and he instructs you to start eating, go ahead. If there is a host, follow his cue. If you are the host, make a comment for guests to start and to enjoy their meals. Even if all have been served, wait until the host or the guest of honor starts to eat.

- Place your napkin on the chair if you need to leave the table, and push your chair in. When you return, the waiter may have refolded your napkin and placed it on the back or the arm of the chair. Remember not to refold the napkin at the end of the meal. Just pick it up from the center and place it loosely on the table to the left of the plate. Do not place it in the plate.

- If time permits, order your meal before you start business. The best situation is to wait for business until after the meal while you are having coffee/drinks, but time constraints and the situation will prevail.

- Don't spread your papers over the table.

- A man should unbutton his jacket at the table but when he stands, rebutton it.

- Refrain from leaning back and do not cross your arms during a business meal.

- Wine may be offered with your meal. If you choose not to have wine with your meal, just tell the wait staff you will not be having any wine or place your fingertips lightly on the rim of the glass when the server approaches. Never turn your glass upside down. Just say, "I will not be having wine today/tonight." To release the bouquet of red wine and brandy, hold the glass by the bowl so the warmth of your hand will enhance the taste. Red wine glasses may be held by the stem or bowl, but white wine and champagne glasses are always held by the stem to keep the chill of the glass.

- Never lift your glassware or cup when someone is pouring. Just let it sit on the table and the wait staff will come to it.
- Always remember to take your cue from the hosts. Once they have lifted their glasses, you may follow.
- See Chapter 5 "Dining and Table Etiquette" for more helpful hints.

Visual Signs for the Wait Staff

- Imagine a clock on your plate. To indicate you are finished eating, place both the knife and fork in about the 10:20 position of a clock with the points at 10 and the handles at 20. The tines of the fork can be up or down, and the blade of the knife should be facing you. If eating American style, the fork tines are up and if eating Continental style, the tines are down. If

you have been eating the course with the fork only, place it tines up in the 10:20 position when finished.

- Another easy sign for the wait staff is to place the fork and knife side by side on the right-hand rim of the plate. The fork is inside the knife, with the fork tines up or down. The blade of the knife should be turned inward.

- If resting while eating in the Continental/ European style, place the knife and fork in an inverted V formation. The blade of the knife should be toward the center of the plate, with the tip of the knife aimed at 12 o'clock and the bottom at 4 o'clock. The tines of the fork should point down and be aimed at 12 o'clock, with the bottom of the handle at 8 o'clock.

- The resting position for eating American style is to place the knife across the top of the plate horizontally with the blade facing toward you and the fork placed diagonally across the plate as similar to the finished position at 10:20 with the tines up.

Table Seating

Many considerations are involved in proper seating, including rank, foreign dignitaries and guests, religious, elderly, military, and executives. The No. 1 principle of seating by rank is to seat the most important person on the host's right and the next most important on the host's left and then to seat the third and fourth most important people on the co-host's right and left.

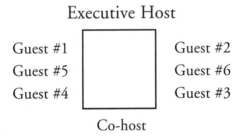

Executive Host

Guest #1		Guest #2
Guest #5		Guest #6
Guest #4		Guest #3

Co-host

Making Introductions

- Always stand for introductions and to shake hands.
- Scenario: At a reception, you are standing, talking to a group of people. A person walks up to talk to you, and you want to introduce him or her to the group but are unsure of someone's name in the group. You should introduce the new person and then ask everyone in the group to introduce themselves.
- Scenario: You approach a table at which there are people already seated. You should move around the table introducing yourself to everyone before you sit down.

- A man is always introduced to a woman. "Mrs. Smith, I'd like you to meet Mr. Albert." The exception is if the man is a head of state, royalty, a church official, or an older man in a high position.
- A young person is introduced to an older person. "Dr. Lauren, I'd like you to meet my nephew, Shaeffer Murphy." "Aunt Evelyn, this is my dear friend, Olivia."
- A less important person is introduced to a prominent person. "Senator Lott, this is Rick Wayne, the precinct chairman."
- If you have a sudden mental block and forget names when making introductions, just make a sincere apology with a big smile. It happens to everyone, so they will forgive you.
- If you see someone is struggling to introduce you, state your name yourself, and offer a handshake.
- If a married woman does not use her husband's name, make sure the names and relationships are clear in the beginning without belaboring the issue.
- My husband and I have a great system. If I see he is struggling to remember the person's name, I immediately extend my hand and introduce myself. It is painless and makes everyone comfortable.

Making a Toast

- Never toast yourself. Stay seated, respond with a thank you, and do not take a drink or hold the glass. If you are standing as part of a reception and you have a drink in your hand, then just stand there, do not motion with the glass and again simply say "thank you."

- Be brief and speak from your heart when you offer a toast. Never have a note card to read the toast. If you can't remember it or memorize it, then it is too long.
- You may return a toast immediately or later near the end of the meal.
- Do not tap or click your glass to get everyone's attention. Just stand and ask for everyone's attention. If there is a band, you can request a change in the tone of music to signal for attention.
- It is not necessary that everyone tap their glasses together to signify the toast. You can motion with the glass or nod to each person and then take a drink.
- A toast can be made with whatever you may be drinking. It does not need to be an alcoholic drink.
- You may make a toast to more than one person. It can be to congratulate or thank an entire department, division, or team.
- When you raise your glass for a toast, do not take it higher than your eyes.
- The host should always be the first one to make the toast.
- If you are entertaining international clients or guests and want to toast them in their native language, be sure to learn the correct pronunciation beforehand. Otherwise, stick to your native tongue.

Buffets

- After everyone is seated and drink orders are taken, the host should gesture for everyone to go to the buffet. If there is no host, a more senior person should make the signal to begin.
- Serve yourself reasonable portions. You can go back for more.
- If an item appears to be in short supply, be conservative. At a restaurant, you can ask the wait staff to replenish, but at a private home, never inquire about more. Usually in a private home, all the food will be displayed at one time.
- Place the serving spoon or fork next to the platter or chafing dish. Do not leave it in the serving dish.
- Don't bring back enough food or desserts for everyone at your table. Bring enough for your own meal unless someone at your table needs assistance or specifically asks you to bring an item.
- At serving stations, limit your requests. Be considerate of the people in line behind you. If you must have a special item, wait until the main rush has already gone through the lines.
- Replace your plate each time you return to a buffet. Never reuse the same plate.
- Don't scrape or stack your plates on the table.
- Be courteous to the people around you. Even though people leave and return to the table, be polite when

eating. If you are the first one back to the table, it is polite to wait for at least one other person to join you before you start to eat.

Receptions

- It's difficult to conduct business and meet someone new when you are constantly eating or drinking and your hands are full, so don't overload your plate.
- Focus on the opportunity to meet people and work the room. Wear your name badge, if appropriate, on your right side.
- See Chapter 4 "Networking: How to Work a Room."

Additional Business Meal Tips

- Mingle. Get to know other guests and your hosts at a function or event.
- When attending a hosted event for your company, spend the time visiting with the company staff that is hosting you. Do not visit for any length of time with those you see daily.
- If your company hosts an employee event, sit with other departments, and introduce yourself to people you do not see regularly. Do not socialize only within your own department.
- If you have the opportunity to order from a menu, order what you normally would when you are paying for the meal. Be conservative. Don't order highly

priced items or specialty drinks. Never ask to take food home when you are attending a business meal.

- Follow the lead of your hosts. If they order smaller meals, you don't have to have just a cup of soup but don't order a four-course meal either. Also, if they pass on dessert and coffee, you should too. Possibly that is a sign they need to return to the office, and there is not enough time for another course.

- Hosting business meals can be challenging for a woman, especially if the guests are men. The female host should be sure to arrange for payment in advance with the restaurant manager, so there will be no issue of who picks up the tab.

- For businesswomen traveling and dining alone, I recommend taking a seat against the wall to be able to see others approaching.

THE POINT IS . . .
As host, plan ahead so you are in control and can ensure your guests' comfort. As a guest, never take advantage of hospitality shown to you.

EIGHT

Handling Difficult Foods

● ● ● ● ● ● ●

The best way to deal with difficult foods is to avoid ordering them, but occasionally you have no choice. Some foods are challenging to deal with gracefully. Here is a short alphabetical list of some problem foods and tips for handling them. Remember, at times it is perfectly correct to eat some foods with your fingers. The general rule is, when in doubt, use cutlery correctly. If you have already touched an item, go ahead and eat it with your fingers.

Apples and Pears

At a formal dinner, when the fruit knife and fork are presented, quarter and peel the fruit, if you wish, then slice into bite-sized pieces and eat with a fork.

Apricots

At a formal dinner, halve the apricot, cut out the pit and eat with a fork.

Artichokes

Artichokes may be served hot or cold. Tear off one leaf at a time, dip the broad end into the accompanying melted butter or Hollandaise sauce, then bring it to your mouth and gently draw the meat out by running the leaf between your teeth. Place the leaves neatly on your plate (if a separate bowl is not provided). You will eventually come to the fuzzy choke, which is inedible. Remove it with your knife and fork to reveal the saucer-shaped artichoke heart, which should be eaten with a knife and fork. Because you have used your fingers to eat the leaves, you should be served a finger bowl when you are finished. During a business meal, this time-consuming and intense ritual draws your attention away from the client, who should be your prime concern, so artichokes would not be an appropriate choice to order.

Asparagus

These are finger foods. It is okay to pick up a stalk at the base, dip the tip into the accompanying sauce and bite off the head. Many people are unaware of this, however, so if your client uses a knife and fork to cut asparagus, by all means do the same. Individual tongs are sometimes brought in with asparagus, and they may be used instead of your fingers to grasp the base. When asparagus is overcooked and soft, it is best to use your knife and fork. Any part of the base that is too tough to chew is left on the side of the plate.

Avocado

If it is served cut in half with the pit removed, eat it with a spoon. If peeled, cut up and served with a salad, it is eaten with a fork.

Bacon

The correct way to eat bacon is with a fork. If it is extremely crisp and dry, fingers may be used.

Bananas

In a formal setting, the banana should be peeled, cut into slices, and eaten with a fork.

Berries

In a formal setting, berries are eaten with a spoon. A large berry, such as a strawberry, may be eaten with a fruit fork and knife. If berries are served whole with the hull attached, you may hold each at the hull and dip the berry into the accompanying sauce, cream or sugar. To eat a giant chocolate-dipped strawberry, insert the fork into the flesh near the stem and slice the berry vertically several times and cut off the stem. Do this carefully, so you don't destroy the chocolate coating.

Bread

When you are served an uncut loaf of bread, you may cut or break off your own slice then pass the loaf to the person to your right. The host may decide to cut the entire loaf and then pass the cut bread to the others at the table.

Butter

Use the clean dinner fork to bring the butter to your plate; use the butter knife to spread butter on bread (one bite at a time). Butter is put on a baked potato with your fork, not your knife.

Canapes

Served before a meal, they are finger foods; served at the table, they are eaten with a fork.

Caviar

Spread caviar on toast with a knife, hold the toast with your fingers and take one bite at a time.

Celery. Radishes. and Pickles

Take relishes off the service plate with your fingers, place them on your dinner plate and eat them with your fingers.

If there are tongs on the service plate, use them to move these relishes to your plate.

Cherries or Other Fruits with Pits

If these fruits are eaten with the fingers in an informal setting, remove the pit from your mouth into your hand and place the pit on the edge of your plate. At a formal setting, when served in a dessert, a spoon is used. Bring the spoon to your mouth, put the pit into the spoon, and place it on the edge of your plate.

Chicken or Fowl

Unless you are at a picnic or barbecue, chicken is not a finger food. Use your knife and fork.

Chops (of any kind)

The chicken rule applies. Although the tastiest meat may be closest to the bone, if you can't cut it off with your knife and fork, the meat must remain on your plate.

Clams

Whether they are baked or served on the half shell, clams are eaten in one bite. Use the oyster fork to pick up the clam. You may then pick up the shell and drink the remaining clam juice. For steamed clams, open the shell and with your fingers pull away the black outer skin covering the neck. Holding the neck, dip the clam into the accompanying broth or melted butter and eat it in one mouthful. This complicated, time-consuming, and potentially messy ritual makes steamers inadvisable at a business meal.

Corn on the Cob

Corn on the cob is served only in a very informal setting. Hold it with both hands and butter just a few rows at a time. This food is never served on formal occasions. In Europe, corn on the cob is considered food for livestock.

Crackers

Be cautious with crackers. Do not break them into soup and do not hold a cracker in one hand and the soup spoon in the other. Treat crackers like bread.

Éclair

It's best to eat all pastries with a fork.

Eggs

To eat a boiled egg in a cup, crack the shell gently with a knife, lift off the shell, and place it on the edge of the plate. Steady the egg cup with one hand and eat the egg with the other hand, using a spoon.

Escargots (snails)

Escargots are usually served with a special pair of tongs and a double-pronged fork. Grip the snail shell in the tongs, and pull out the snail with the fork. If there is bread at the table, it is perfectly correct (and delicious) to dip the bread into the garlic sauce after you have eaten the snails. This is another inadvisable selection for business meals.

Fish

A fish fillet is eaten with a fish fork. If fish is presented whole, you can ask the server to fillet it, but if you have to do it yourself, use the fish knife (if provided) or your dinner knife. Start by cutting just behind the head. Then slice down the length of the fish along the skeletal cage. Using your knife and fork, fold back the top half of the fish, exposing the bone. Lift the entire bone structure out and place it on the side of your plate. Then eat the fish with your fish fork. If you find a small bone in a bite, take it from your mouth with your thumb and forefinger and place it on the edge of your plate. Again, this may be too much of a procedure for a business meal.

French Fries

If fries are served with a burger, then use your fingers, but if served in a more formal setting, cut in half and use a fork.

Grapefruit Halves

Section these fruits with your knife to avoid a lot of digging with the spoon. Never squeeze the rind to get the remaining juice.

Hard-shell Crabs and Lobsters

Crack the shell with a nutcracker and use your seafood fork (a small utensil with three tines) to remove the meat. If it is a large piece of meat, cut it with a fork. Pull off the small claws and treat them as if you were drawing liquid through a straw. Stuffed lobster is eaten with a knife and fork. This is another food that you may wish to avoid ordering when entertaining a client.

Lemons

Cup a lemon in your hand to avoid squirting anyone as you squeeze it over tea or seafood.

Mussels

Mussels may be removed from the shell with a fork, dipped into the sauce, and eaten in one bite. In a more informal setting, you may pick up the shell, scoop a little of the juice with it, and suck the mussel and juice directly off the shell. Place the empty shells in a bowl or plate that should be provided.

Oysters

There are various ways to prepare and eat oysters. If on the half shell, steady the shell on the plate with one hand, and with the other hand use an oyster fork to lift out the oyster, which you then place in your mouth whole and chew, if necessary. You may pick up the shell and drink the juice after you have eaten the oyster. Oysters in a stew are eaten with a spoon. Fried oysters are eaten with a knife and fork.

Parfait

Start at the top using the long parfait spoon usually served with this dessert and inch your way down to the syrup at the bottom. Don't try to stir the syrup or fruits to the top.

Pasta

Pasta can present problems. My first suggestion is to simply cut it to be safe. Otherwise, using your fork, separate a few strands and twirl the fork against the edge of the plate to gather the strands onto it. Make sure the bite is not too large and unmanageable. It is difficult to avoid dripping sauce or having problems with pasta, so if you have a choice, don't order it at a business meal.

Petits Fours

These small cakes are finger foods and are eaten in small bites. If they are presented on paper wrappers, take the wrapper from the serving dish with your selection.

Potato, Baked

Cut an X in the top, squeeze the potato slightly with your fingers, then add butter and/or sour cream. If you add butter, use your fork. Don't try to convert the inside into mashed potatoes. If you want to eat the skin, cut it into small pieces with a knife and fork.

Shrimp

If the tails are left on, then eat shrimp with your fingers. Shrimp cocktail should be eaten with a seafood fork, in two bites if large, or you can put the shrimp on a plate and cut them with a knife and fork.

Sushi and Sashimi

Eat sushi pieces whole if they are small enough, or cut them with a knife and fork or with the ends of chopsticks. It is also proper to use your fingers to eat sushi.

Tomatoes, Cherry

It's difficult to chase cherry tomatoes around your plate and they usually are too large to eat whole, so it is best to use a knife and fork to cut them into pieces.

Watermelon

Use a spoon when watermelon is in small balls. Otherwise, use a fork and knife. Put the seeds in the palm of your hand and then transfer them to your plate.

THE POINT IS . . .
Don't create problems for yourself or your guests by ordering difficult foods for a business dinner.

NINE

Working in a Home Office

• • • • • • • •

Is working out of your home really for you? If you want to start your own company, it could be smarter financially to work from your home and avoid the overhead expenses of a building or an office suite. Perhaps your company is downsizing or is running out of office space and has asked you to work from your home. Moving to a home or virtual office is a major transition. You need to review the advantages and disadvantages of working independently, establish a start-up budget, get organized, and create routines for working from home.

Disadvantages of Working from a Home Office

- No support staff, or at least not at arm's length
- Smaller storage space
- No heavy-duty copy machine
- No in-house postal service
- Less socializing with coworkers
- The cost of setting up your own office
- Having to be everything: the receptionist, switch-board operator, administrative assistant, mail room

person, head of purchasing, chief of finance, customer service, and sales and marketing staff
- More self-discipline and less guidance
- The challenge of separating your personal life from professional business during the day
- The perception by others that you are not really working

Advantages of Working from a Home Office

- Independence
- Efficiency of working with fewer interruptions
- Being in control of your own schedule
- No dress code
- No office politics
- No commute time and no traffic to fight
- Low overhead costs after start-up

Finding/Making Space for a Home Office

- Many people think they will just convert a part of their dining room or use the little alcove in their bedroom for an office. Chances are this will not work. You need to evaluate your home and decide if you have the necessary space. You need room for a permanent desk, chair, computer hook up, file cabinets, separate phone lines, fax machine, printer, storage space, sufficient electrical outlets and good lighting. Plus, it's an advantage if you can work away from major distractions.

- If clients need to come to your home office for a meeting, will you have a separate entrance to your office or will they need to walk through most of your home to get to your office or meeting space? You need to decide. It might be better to meet at their office or at another convenient location.
- Do you need to create a completely new area by constructing a new space, converting an existing area, or remodeling a particular room, basement, or perhaps a larger closet? It is amazing what you can do with existing areas. The costs and the time of building or remodeling must be factored into your plans for a starting date, as well as your budget.
- A consultation with a professional office organizer may save you time, money, and energy in the long run.

Getting Organized in Your new Office

When you find the best space in your home, you must get organized. Your new office at home may have less space than your corporate office. Even if you are fortunate and have a large area, the space must be designed properly. Take your time in the beginning and work out a floor plan that fits your space, needs, and budget. But, you say, you must get moved into your new office immediately and start working. Believe me, the time you invest initially will save you time in the long run. Begin with a good plan. After you have found the right space for your office, you must:

- Set up the office so it is functional.
- Have a plan. It may take a while to create this plan, but think through the process, and make sure you select what fits your needs and office space.
- Consider the costs involved. Do you have most of your equipment and furniture, or do you need to buy it? If so, then consider your budget. If your budget is limited, then buy the office equipment first and save the furniture for later. But make sure you consider private phone lines, a good office phone, computer/ printers and fax machine. Do not buy office equipment knowing that within a year you will need to upgrade. Possibly your corporate office will provide equipment for you, or you can purchase equipment at reduced rates. But be aware that the desk that worked in your big corporate office may overwhelm your new home office.
- Use a grid to chart out the space for your furnishings. Measure exactly how much space you have, and then chart it on the grid. Don't buy equipment and furniture and hope it fits in your office. The grid or floor plan will allow you to move around templates of a desk, chair, and file cabinets, so you can see the actual setup.
- Organize and find a place for your files and office supplies. Get rid of old files and unnecessary items. Don't just move them around. If you don't need them, throw them away. If you move them to another area, you will have the same problem later.

- When planning your office space, think efficiency and organization. If you operate professionally, you will work professionally.

- If your second office is your car, organize it so you can operate efficiently. Keep a container to hold files that can easily be accessed for your next meeting. Don't attempt to talk on a cell phone or work as you drive.

Estimating Equipment and Initial Setup Costs

Costs for setting up your office will vary tremendously. You may be starting with absolutely nothing or may already own some equipment and need to buy some items. Decide what is critical to begin your office and how much you can afford to spend. Buy only the absolute essentials in the beginning and then add items as you need them or can afford them. Always look for sales at office supply stores and computer stores. Below is a very basic list of what you may need and the range of costs to purchase these items.

Bookshelves	$50–$200
Chair(s)	$75–$200+
Computer (desktop)	$1,000–$2,000
Computer desk	$125–$300
Credenza/Work table	$100–$300
Desk	$150–$400+
Fax machine	$200–$600
File cabinets	$100–$500

Floor mat	$25–$125
DSL lines	$150/line (varies by location)
Lamps	$15–$200
Laptop computer	$1,000–$3,000
Phone lines (2-3)	$150–$250 (plus answering service)
Phone(s)	Monthly charges (plus initial installation)
Printer (color/B&W)	$100–$300
Scanner	$75–$400
Stationery/Business cards	$50–$1,500
Web site construction	$500–$2,000+

Of course, costs can vary widely depending on your needs and your tastes. You may already have or want to purchase other items for your office including additional furniture, a clock, radio, waste paper baskets, calculator, personal digital assistant (such as PalmPilot™), postage scale and meter, electric pencil sharpener, or electric stapler.

Purchasing Office Supplies

Working from home takes away the advantage of walking into the corporate office supply room and taking what you need. Now you must evaluate your initial needs, buy items that must be replenished, as well as items that you will need to buy only once. Some of the supplies include:

Binders and tab dividers for proposals
Computer disks
Computer ink cartridges
Cover stock paper
Dictionary
Expense reports
File folders
Hanging folders with tabs
Highlighters and markers
Hole punch (single, double, three-hole)
Invoices/Petty cash book
Labels (folders, mailing)
Laser printer paper
Legal pads
Mailing envelopes
Manila folders
Message stamps (paid, to be paid, file)
Note pads
Overnight delivery envelopes and mailing labels
Paper (copy, computer, fax)
Paper clips (various sizes)
Pens/Pencils
Rubber bands
Scissors
Stamps
Stapler, staples, and staple remover
Sticky notes
Tape and dispenser
Thesaurus

Your specific type of work and office space will determine the supplies you need. Keep supplies as well stocked as possible. Watch for sales at office supply stores, but don't buy something just because it is on sale. Keep a list handy to check off when you need supplies, and take it with you when you go to the office supply store. It is more efficient to work from a list. Remember your storage space and try to buy only what you need.

What Belongs on Your Desk?

The answer is as little as possible. Some people insist on a clean desk and some just love to work in clutter. It's hard to change either person, but clutter can and will interfere with your productivity. The following are some desktop guidelines:

- The computer is the centerpiece of the desk. Position it first.
- Your printer can be on or next to your desk.
- Put the fax machine on an extended desktop or close to your desk.
- You may need a lamp on your desk in addition to overhead lights or if you have no overhead lights.
- Keep on your desk only items that you use daily.
- Keep close at hand items that you use weekly.
- Keep pens, tablets, stapler, staple remover, tape, etc., organized and ready to use.
- Organize items to work to your advantage. If you are right-handed, put your phone on the left side so you

can take notes, or vice versa for left-handers. Headsets for phones are also great tools.

What Belongs in Desk Drawers and File Cabinets?

The first thing you need to do is get organized. Are there stacks and stacks of papers on your desk, the floor, and every possible space in your office? Do you throw them away or file them? Do you need additional file cabinets, shelves, or stacking bins? Do you have space for them?

Start with what you have. Go through your drawers one at a time, and you'll be amazed at what you can discard. Do you really need that old file? Do you really need those old magazines or articles? Probably not.

- If you haven't used an item in a year, it is pretty safe to throw it away.
- Toss out things that don't work anymore, such as old pens and highlighters.
- Use desk trays to organize drawers and maximize the space you have. Put paper clips in one section of the organizer so they are in one area and easy for you to reach and use instantly. Don't mix clips with staples and rubber bands.
- Use files to hold your paper, stationery, fax cover sheets, etc. This keeps them neat and convenient.
- Remember, with everything stored on your computer, many paper files can be eliminated.

You will save so much time by being organized and not looking for a certain sheet of stationery or a paper clip. Unfortunately those stacks of paper seem to continue growing, so staying organized can be a continuing challenge.

Balancing Professional and Personal Life

When you work in a corporate office, your personal life is secondary to work from 8 AM until 5 PM. But when your office is in your home, it can become difficult to separate your personal life from your work. Set guidelines and be disciplined enough to keep the two as separate as possible.

- The first step is to move your office away from the busy part of your home where there is traffic and noise.
- If you have children at home with a sitter/nanny, rules about their care away from your office must be set and adhered to.
- Keep the house duties on hold until after your work hours or limit yourself to quick, simple chores like tossing a load of clothes in the washer or dryer.
- Remember, you can't be shopping or playing golf all day and achieve your business goals.

It is basically impossible to keep the professional and personal completely separated, but you must focus on work during business hours.

Daily Routine for a Home Office

When you worked in the corporate world, you would wake up at the same time each morning and go through your usual rituals to get ready for work. Then you would either drive or ride the bus/rail to get to your office. With an office at home, you can wake up and go directly to work. But there are disadvantages to being a few steps down the hallway from your office. You should develop a pattern similar to what you had before, just minus leaving your house.

- Schedule a regular wake-up time.
- Set routine office hours.
- Take your shower and do your normal morning rituals, in case someone calls for a last-minute appointment. You will be ready.
- Schedule a lunch time, whether you are going out or staying home.
- Try to schedule your appointments not to coincide with heavy traffic in the morning or evening.
- Try to schedule appointments on the same day or back-to-back so you are not making excessive trips to and from your office.
- Don't forget to make regular backups of your computer and personal data devices.
- Stay focused on your work, but leave time to take a break.

- Don't eat breakfast or lunch at your desk.
- Schedule one full day a week to stay in your office and get things done. Try to pick the day of the week when calls are a little slower and fewer appointments are usually booked. If such a day doesn't exist, at least let your voice mail answer your calls for half a day while you get caught up.
- Be disciplined about your routine. For some, it is too easy to work all hours of the day and night because work is close at hand. For others, it may be easy to go play that game of golf during the day and then plan to get caught up with work at night.
- Take off one day a month and enjoy it out of your office.
- Make sure you have two phone lines into your home/office. Let your personal phone line go into the answering machine.
- Learn to say no. Some have a problem saying no and accept more projects, join more committees, and sign up to do more programs, thinking it might create future business, when, in fact, it could hurt. Taking on too much jeopardizes the quality of your work. Choose extra projects selectively. Make sure they will work for you and your career.

Postal Service

You may want to secure a special postal service account with a service such as the UPS Stores. For a monthly fee, you can get a post office box or suite number. Although having to go to this location daily or every other day is a disadvantage, there are many advantages as follows:

- Your professional mail is delivered separately from your personal mail.
- Business contacts will not know your home address.
- A suite address gives your company a professional image.
- The postal service will accept packages and sign for them.
- You may get access to faster and larger fax and copy machines.
- Services such as overnight shipping may be available.

Receipts/Income

It is critical to start a filing system solely for your receipts. For almost a year, I tossed my receipts into one box. I thought that was pretty organized because they were all in one place. But at the end of the year, I still needed to sort them to prepare my income tax. Now I report my income tax quarterly, and that is so much better for my organization.

- Use separate credit cards for business and personal expenditures. It is easier to keep the two separated for tax purposes and reporting business expenses.
- Keep track of all your expenses and receipts.
- Start a file system and automatically file your receipts

to keep accurate records so you will know how much money you are spending throughout the year.

- Purchase a software program such as QuickBooks, so your accounting system looks professional and the checks are typed and recorded.

- When you travel, carry an expense report that can easily be transferred into your financial system, and an envelope to hold all of your receipts.

- At the bottom of each receipt make sure to write the purpose of the expense and, if a client was involved, include the name, company, and purpose of the meeting/meal.

- Keep a form in your car to record mileage at the beginning and end of your business trips. Don't rely on your memory.

- If finance is not your strongest asset, you may need to hire a CPA/bookkeeper to assist you with setting up your finances, handling your income tax withdrawals, and reporting your income tax. It may cost a little more but in the long run, it will be beneficial. You'll save time and frustration and have support if you are audited.

Suggested Files for a Financial System

Advertising/Promotion
Bank loans
Bank statements
   (cancelled checks)
Car/Mileage/Tolls/Parking
Charge accounts

Educational material
   (tapes, books)
Educational seminars/
   Conventions
Gifts
Hotel expenses

Insurance

Investments (pension, profit-sharing, SEP)

Invoices

Legal costs

Marketing

Meals and entertainment

Memberships/Dues

Office equipment

Office supplies

Postage (including box rentals)

Printing

Rent

Salaries/Contract labor

Stationery/Business cards

Tax deductions/Charities

Telephone (office and cell)

Travel (airfare, car rental)

Utilities

Staying in Touch with the Corporate World

It is important to be involved with professional organizations and to stay in contact with your peers. Some people fear if they work from home, others will forget about them, and their value in the job market will be diminished. If anything, it has been proven that people who work from their homes are more productive and reach their goals and quotas. And if you conduct all your business at the highest professional level, many of your clients and contacts will never be aware that you work from a home office.

THE POINT IS . . .
Organization, self-discipline, and balance are the keys to working successfully from a home office.

TEN

Packing for Business Travel

———————— ● ● ● ● ● ● ● ————————

After traveling for business for over two decades, my dream was to one day take exactly what I need for every trip and nothing more. But doing that takes planning, the right luggage, check lists, and knowing your itinerary.

Luggage

The luggage you use depends on your travel schedule and your needs. Luggage has changed drastically over the years to accommodate all kinds of travelers. The biggest advancement is that luggage is now soft-sided, lighter, and on wheels.

- Shop around for the best deals, but don't overlook quality and durability.
- Consider how frequently you travel and whether most of that travel is by air, train, or ship.
- Consider how you will travel once you reach your destination—by rental car, taxi, shuttle bus—and how many bags you will want to carry with you.
- Do you want your luggage to fit in the overhead compartment of an airplane?

- Do you prefer to fold, roll, or hang your garments?
- Do you prefer soft-sided or hard-sided luggage?
- Do you prefer to carry your luggage over your shoulder, pull it, or hold it by handles?

If you plan to add to your luggage, think about the color, style, and function of each piece. You don't have to buy all your luggage at one time nor do all the pieces of your luggage have to match or come from the same manufacturer. Mine don't! But determine your needs over time and continue to add.

Duffel bags are making a comeback. They are much lighter and have no frame, so they tend to carry a lot more. Now duffle bags have wheels and long handles, so they are equally convenient and generally less expensive than standard luggage.

Identifying Your Luggage

All luggage, including your carry-ons, should be well marked with your name, business telephone number and business address.

- Do you realize how many almost identical black suitcases are going around the carousels at airports? If you have one of those bags, use some type of identifier to help yours stand out. Fasten a belt with your company name around your suitcase or use a large, distinctive luggage tag. When my mother comes to visit, we can spot her luggage immediately because of the brightly colored yarn she ties to the handles. Come up with your own creative distinction. Remember security checks at airports will limit some choices.

- If you work from your home or are retired, use a company name so it gives the impression it is your place of work instead of your home. Do not advertise your home information.

- It is very important to label both the inside and outside of your luggage.

- Take old destination tags off your luggage. Don't make it difficult and time consuming for the airlines when they are trying to send your luggage to your final destination.

Locks

Locks are critical and combination locks may be your best choice. They are a little more secure, and you don't have to worry about keys. You just need to remember the combination. Luggage on airlines must be left unlocked, but other segments of your trip may need locks and tighter security.

Laptops

A laptop/notebook is becoming part of most business travelers' luggage. Now at airports your laptop must go through the conveyor belt for security. Be ready for this at the airport, and make it quick and easy to open, unpack, and repack. Do not send your laptop through the conveyor belt until you walk through. Keep an eye on all of your valuables. With security at a much higher level at all airports, you may be detained and separated from your luggage.

- The case should be light but well padded and easy to carry.
- Make sure it has a shoulder strap in addition to a briefcase handle.
- Have ample compartments inside the case so all items are secured.
- Carry your laptop fully charged and have adapters if needed.
- Make sure your laptop is well marked with luggage tags inside and out. Also have identification labels clearly placed on the laptop.
- Your laptop must fit either in the overhead compartment or under your seat.
- All portable electronic items must remain off during taxi, takeoff, approach, and landing until you arrive at the gate and the seat belt sign is turned off. The flight attendants will advise when you may turn on laptops and other electronic devices.

Your Traveling Briefcase

Keep it lightweight. There are many professional and attractive nylon shoulder bags for both men and women that are much lighter than the standard hard-sided cases. Carry office supplies that you will need during your trip, including notepads, paper clips, pen, pencils, postage stamps, rubber bands, miniature stapler, staples and tape. Always remember to have plenty of business cards, thank-you notes and a calculator, which can be part of a PalmPilot™. My best suggestion is that your briefcase be on wheels. Make sure it fits comfortably under your seat or in the overhead compartment.

How Much to Pack

Do you pack so much that you are not enjoying your travels? If so, you need to repack.

I love to bring a lot of clothes, and I think it is very important to always appear fresh, well dressed, and professional. But there are ways to work around a lot of baggage, look good, and still have enough clothes. Here are a few secrets:

- Always pack your hanging clothes in plastic bags before you put them in a garment bag.
- Always put your shoes in bags to protect them.
- Put socks and underclothes inside the shoes or in empty corners.
- The main key is to bring basic colors so you can mix and match. A basic top or shirt can be reused with different jackets, and jewelry or scarves can change the look of an outfit and give you two for the space of one.

- Layer-pack your garment bag. Start with a blouse or shirt on a hanger, put a dress or sweater over it and then put a jacket on top. Enclose all in a plastic bag. (More on this later in the chapter.)
- A few basic shoes will suffice instead of eight or nine pairs, which, I admit, I have carried before I wised up.

Reasons for Overpacking

- You don't want to leave anything behind.
- You are afraid you won't have enough clothes.
- You aren't sure how to dress or what the weather will be, so you bring extra outfits just in case.
- You throw your clothes together the day of the trip or maybe just hours before the trip.
- You forget to go to the cleaners so you don't have exactly what you need.
- You pack an iron and a hair dryer when the hotel has them in the room for you. Call the hotel to ask if these items are provided, so you can leave yours at home.

To Carry On or to Check?

Some people would never consider checking their bags. For them one good carry-on is enough. For others, it would never work.

- There are all kinds of carry-ons. A carry-on garment bag works great to keep your suits and dresses hanging, and you can put other necessities in the pockets. Garment bags will not fit under your seat, but they will fit in the overhead bin or in the front of the cabin.

- Probably the most popular carry-on is a suitcase with wheels. The only problem is that some people pack them so full and heavy that they struggle to pick them up and put them in the overhead compartment, or they are bulging so much, they won't fit. The normal size is 45 linear inches (length + width + height) and no more than 40 pounds for the overhead bin or under your seat. It can be any dimensions totaling 45 inches, but it needs to fit easily. It could be 22 x 14 x 9 or 20 x 16 x 9.

- Other carry-ons include duffel bags, totes, and travel packs. They can all work, depending on what and how much you plan to put inside.

- Remember the space at your feet is yours, but the space over your head is shared. People do become possessive of the overhead space. So when your row is called to board the plane, you might want to be up front to secure that space.

- Each airline has rules regarding acceptable items that may be taken on a plane, either as a carry-on or with checked luggage. It is advisable to check in advance rather than to have an item confiscated or held for your return.

- Before you travel, check with each airline about the exact number of carry-on bags allowed and the size requirements. Remember if you exceed the allotted free baggage allowance for either checked or carried luggage, you may be charged for the additional pieces. Each airline varies on these charges. The pricing can be anywhere from $75 to $175 for additional or oversized baggage.

- You also should consider how you will carry your luggage after you leave the plane, bus, or train.

Suggested Items for Your Carry-on

- Breakables
- Camera and film
- Clothing (change of underclothes)
- Keys
- Laptop or other electronic equipment
- Medicines and prescriptions
- Personal documents
- Snacks and bottled water
- Toiletries (toothbrush, toothpaste, deodorant)
- Valuables (jewelry and cash)
- Work materials

Packing Strategies

From the time you start to plan your trip or receive the first itinerary for a convention or meeting, you need to start preparing what you will take. Consider the weather, the dress codes, schedule of activities, and the purposes of your trip.

- Will the dress code be casual, business casual, business, or formal or a combination of all of this? The advance information may specify no jeans or shorts. So plan your wardrobe accordingly.

- When I receive the itinerary, I always make an extra copy and write beside each event or program what I will wear, including my shoes, jewelry, and belts. When I pull my clothes, I do it by outfits. That way, I don't forget my belt, earrings, or other accessories.

- For a four-day meeting, with seminars each day and activities each night, you need eight outfits. You don't need to pack eight different outfits but possibly only five basics that can be mixed and matched to give you eight different looks. If you plan to wear slacks to all events, instead of packing eight pairs of pants, pack three or four and be creative. Make selections that can be dressed up or down. It becomes fun, and, I promise, you will look different each time.

- If you love your new lime outfit and must take it, you'll probably need another pair of shoes in addition to the basic ones already packed, a different belt and perhaps a different purse.

- Men have it a little easier but not much. A few pair of basic pants, some shirts, jackets, basic shoes, and belts, and you are ready to go. But don't take it too lightly. Your dress and appearance are important, too. So the rules still apply to you. Stick to basic colors for the base outfits, shoes, and belts and then just build around them.

- A caution to both men and women is that not all

clothes mix and match well. Watch your fabrics, weights, and colors.

- Don't forget to decide what you will wear for your travel days. If you need to go straight to your business meeting, women should wear a knit or material that travels well, and men should choose slacks that won't show every wrinkle. Or you may need to take a carry-on bag and change before going to your meeting.

Accessories

- Simple is beautiful. Pack smart and minimize the jewelry you carry. Again, if you stick to two or three basic colors for your wardrobe, fewer accessories will be needed.
- Be very careful about jewelry when you travel. You risk losing your jewelry, leaving it behind, or having it stolen. Sometimes when you return to your room between meetings or events, you change quickly and open your jewelry pouch. You could drop something or inadvertently forget to put it away.
- Take jewelry that can be worn with most of your outfits, or pack jewelry that can be replaced easily.
- Unless you never take them off, don't travel with heirlooms, antiques, or sentimental items.
- Many hotels have a safe in the room. Use it or check with the front desk or concierge, and ask to use their safe. The disadvantage is having to ask them repeatedly to open it to retrieve an item or to store something.

Preparations List

Don't wait until the last minute to prepare for a trip. Some travel will need more attention and preparation, particularly international trips. Planning ahead will allow you to leave on time and be relaxed and ready for the travel and the actual business part of the trip.

- Pick up your clothes from the dry cleaner.
- Do laundry.
- Replenish your toiletries kits.
- Get traveler's checks or foreign currency.
- Make sure you have enough small bills for tipping at the airport and the hotel.
- Secure luggage tags on your luggage inside and out.
- Get tissue paper and plastic bags to wrap your clothes so they arrive crisp and unwrinkled.
- Don't forget extra resealable bags to hold toiletries or wet clothes, such as a bathing suit.

Several days before I leave on a trip, I place my luggage in my walk-in closet so I can place my travel kits on the bottom and start placing items little by little, so packing is not a chore.

Ready to Roll or Fold

Everyone has preferences in packing. I use a little bit of everything. I'm not a big roller except for my T-shirts or casual clothes. The rest I fold or hang. Do whatever works best for you and the type of luggage you use. Here are some pointers:

- Rolling works for both light and heavy clothing and is really great for a duffle bag. Just lay the item face down and fold in the sleeves. Then start at the bottom and roll up. Keep the article smooth as you roll, so you are not creating wrinkles. The collar will be on the outside of the roll. You can roll anything. If you have a pair of slacks or jeans, hold them by the cuffs and lay them down. Make sure you get out all the wrinkles. Start to roll up from the cuffs. You may want to pad more delicate items, such as blouses, shirts, skirts, or dresses with plastic bags or tissue paper and then roll. If something is flimsy, fold it in half lengthwise over another garment to pad the crease and roll them together.

- Interlocking fold means the clothes interlock. First lay down a skirt or a pair of slacks across an open suitcase from top to bottom. Then place a sweater on top of the pants or skirt but place it left to right. Allow the arms of the sweater to drape over the sides of the suitcase. Take the top part of the slacks or skirt and put it over the top of the sweater. Fold the sweater arms in over this, and then fold the bottom part of the sweater and bottom part of the slacks or skirt over everything. Now you have a very neat little stack of clothes. You can repeat this process as many times as you wish and, I promise, your clothes will be wrinkle-free. You will have a lot of space along the sides and in the corners to place your underwear, socks and shoes. Remember to stuff those shoes and keep them in bags. Stuffing your shoes will not only save space but also keep the shape of your shoes.

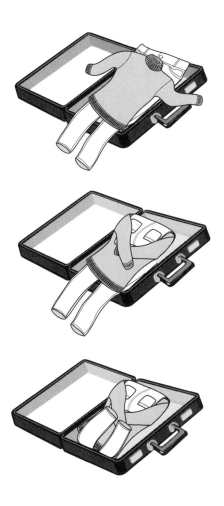

- Many people use a systematic, chronological approach, and it is a tremendous time-saver. You can roll or fold, but place your clothes in the suitcase in the order you will wear them. So the first day's clothes will be on top, and the second day will be next. What a great time-saver when you reach your destination, but you must be organized when you pack. I think this is a grand idea, but I like to unpack my clothes when I reach my hotel room, even if I am staying only two days. If it is just an overnight trip, I will likely leave my clothes in the suitcase, since there are so few items.

Getting the Hang of Garment Bags

I prefer garment bags because as soon as I get to the hotel, I like to take my clothes out and hang them in the closet. Use lots of plastic bags and tissue paper. You can put a dry cleaner's bag over the hanger first to give it a little cushioning and then cover the garments with another plastic bag.

- If I am taking a blouse, I stuff the sleeves with tissue paper to keep it from creasing—the more padding the better. Use hangers that have slight padding so your clothes will not slip off. There is nothing worse than getting to your destination and finding all your clothes at the bottom of the bag.
- When you place your items in the garment bag, start with the longest on the bottom, your more delicate

items in the middle, and then the remaining items on top. Even though they are all in plastic bags, add a few more bags before closing the zipper. This will provide additional padding and protect the top clothes from the zipper or straps.

- A space-saving trick is layering or stacking your clothes on hangers. Start by placing a blouse or T-shirt on a hanger. Then add your dress or jacket. Obviously, it would be great to stack actual outfits so they will be ready to go. Remember the plastic bags and tissue paper. If you have a pair of slacks, cover the pant hanger bar with a T-shirt or sweater first and then lay the pants over that to prevent a sharp crease in the pants. You can add a tie over the pants. On top of all of this can go a shirt and a jacket. When you reach the hotel, you can unstack clothes and place them on individual hangers provided by the hotel.

- I do not recommend putting toiletries in a garment bag. If it is tossed or thrown to the ground, the chances are a lot greater that items could burst, leak, or spill. Also do not place anything of value in the outside pockets of a garment bag unless you can lock every zipper and compartment.

- Some airlines will provide a garment bag box to be checked if you request one. But when they are really busy, they do not want to take the time to assemble one and have you place your garment bag inside. Still, it is worth asking. Make sure you print your name clearly on the outside of the box on both sides.

Ties

There is nothing worse than a tie that is badly wrinkled. One way to prevent wrinkles is to roll ties and place them in a jacket pocket. You can also lay them flat inside the sleeve of a jacket or lay them over the pants on the hanger bar. Carrying cases made especially for ties are great for travelers (and a good gift for the guy who has everything).

Travel Toiletries Kits

I have three kits that are always packed and ready to go. One I hook on the back of the door in the bathroom as soon as I arrive; it holds my toothpaste and all those necessary items. Another kit holds all my hair items including a comb, brush, small mirror and my hair dryer, if I need one. The last one keeps my other toiletries all in plastic bags. As soon as I return from a trip, I replenish each of these bags and keep them with my suitcases. I move them to whatever suitcase I am taking for the next trip, and I am ready to go. Hotels provide some amenities such as shampoo and conditioner. If you prefer particular brands, then pack your own in travel sizes. The following is an inventory of items for your travel kits:

Aspirin
Comb and brush
Conditioner

Contact lens supplies
Cotton swabs/balls
Dental floss

Deodorant

Facial cream/Cleanser

First-aid kit

Hair dryer

Hairspray

Hand lotion

Insect repellent

Makeup

Makeup remover

Moisturizer

Mouthwash

Nail supplies

Razor

Sewing kit

Shampoo

Shaving cream

Spot remover (small bottle
    of detergent or Woolite)

Sunscreen

Tissues

Toothbrush

Toothpaste

Tweezers

Wipes

If you purchase small plastic bottles to fill with your products, remember not to fill them to the top. The changes in air pressure during a flight could cause containers to leak. Put all of these items in a resealable bag.

Checklists

When I started preparing this book, I asked several people for checklists and received many great samples. But the best one came from my friend Laurie Sprouse. It was the most complete list I had ever seen. So, with my gratitude, here is Laurie's list, with just a few adjustments:

DOCUMENTS
- ○ AAA card
- ○ Airline tickets
- ○ Check receipt
- ○ Copy of documents
- ○ Driver's license
- ○ Health insurance card
- ○ Itinerary
- ○ Passport (and a copy of the front page)
- ○ Rental car voucher
- ○ Train tickets
- ○ Visa

MONEY
- ○ Cash
- ○ Credit cards
- ○ Foreign currency
- ○ Traveler's checks

COMPUTER
- ○ Adapter
- ○ Car adapter
- ○ CDs
- ○ Cord
- ○ E-mail information
- ○ Extra batteries
- ○ Fax modem
- ○ Phone line/Adapters

WALKMAN AND HEADPHONES
- ○ Batteries
- ○ Blank cassettes
- ○ Cassettes or CDs

COLD WEATHER
- ○ Gloves
- ○ Hat/Ski headband
- ○ Overcoat
- ○ Scarf/Muffler
- ○ Sweater
- ○ Thermals

MISCELLANEOUS
- ○ Appointment information/PalmPilot™ (names, addresses, phone numbers)
- ○ Calling cards/Dialing information
- ○ Personal phone numbers and addresses

BUSINESS COLLATERAL
- ○ Brochures
- ○ Business cards
- ○ Business gifts
- ○ Information packets
- ○ Picture book
- ○ Videos

CARRY-ONS
- ○ Airplane pillow
- ○ Aspirin/Pain reliever
- ○ Bottled water
- ○ Cell phone
- ○ Ear plugs/Mask
- ○ Sleeping pills

BOOKS/MAPS
- ○ Guide books
- ○ Phrase book
- ○ Reading materials
- ○ Road maps

SUPPLIES
- ○ Business note paper
- ○ Calculator
- ○ Envelopes
- ○ Expense report forms
- ○ File folders
- ○ Highlighters
- ○ Notepads
- ○ Paperclips
- ○ Pens, staplers, staples
- ○ Rubber bands
- ○ Stamps
- ○ Thank-you notes

CLOTHING
- ○ Bathing suit/Cover-up
- ○ Belts/Suspenders
- ○ Business suits/Dresses
- ○ Coat/Jacket/Raincoat
- ○ Formal/Cocktail attire
- ○ Golf attire (if needed)
- ○ Handkerchiefs
- ○ Jackets/Sport coat
- ○ Jeans/Shorts
- ○ Jewelry/Accessories
- ○ Shirts (dress, casual)
- ○ Shoes (business, casual, athletic)
- ○ Slacks (dress, casual)
- ○ Sleepwear/Slippers
- ○ Socks/Hosiery
- ○ Sweaters/Turtlenecks
- ○ Ties/Scarves
- ○ Underwear
- ○ Work-out gear

PERSONAL

○ Artificial sweetener

○ Chewing gum/Mints

○ Curling iron and adapter

○ Eyeglasses/Contact lens solutions

○ Face lotions

○ Hair dryer and adapter

○ Ibuprofen/Aspirin

○ Snacks

○ Sunglasses

○ Tea/Hot chocolate

○ Travel toiletries kits

○ Umbrella

○ Vitamins, herbs, cold medications

Notes for Traveling Abroad

- Have an up-to-date passport. Be sure it will be valid when you are ready to return home. It can take four to five weeks to receive a new passport and three to four weeks to renew one. If you don't have this much time, you can visit a U.S. Passport Office, and they will handle your request for an additional fee.

- Be aware of any visas you may need.

- Do you need any inoculations for your destination? Plan this well in advance. It may take weeks to receive all the necessary shots.

- It is essential to purchase electrical adapters before you leave on an international trip. Most countries use a standard 220-volt current, but in the United States, we use 110 volts. You can find adapters in any travel store or in most major department stores.

• Keep all documents together in a pouch or a specific travel case that you always have with you. These should include your passport, visa, copies of your prescriptions, traveler's checks, credit card numbers and important phone numbers. It is highly recommended that you also keep a copy of the first page of your passport. These are critical items and when you carry them, keep them close to your body and concealed.

Shipping Luggage

At times, I will have back-to-back business trips. Of course, they inevitably will be different types of trips to different climates. You can ship luggage to your hotel via a parcel service, such as USPS, UPS, or FedEx. Allow enough time for it to arrive ahead of you and alert the hotel to be expecting it. The hotel can store it and have it waiting for you upon arrival. It is convenient and easy. You can also ship home a box of convention/trade show materials, gifts, or a suitcase of laundry to avoid having to check or carry extra baggage on your return trip.

While You're Gone

Review the tips in Chapter 11 "Being Safe at Home and on the Road." Don't forget about your mail, newspapers, keeping lights on, and giving the impression that you are still at home. Trust a neighbor or a good friend to keep an eye on your home or apartment. Also remember to use the "Out of Office" function on your computer to provide information about how you may be reached.

THE POINT IS . . .
Efficient packing means knowing how and what to pack as well as using the right luggage for the trip. Checklists and systems help simplify your business trips.

ELEVEN

Being Safe at Home and on the Road

●●●●●●●

Personal safety and security is important to everyone. After all, if you and your loved ones are not safe, nothing else matters much, does it? "It can't happen here" is an excuse that is not applicable anymore. You can be unsafe at work, on the road, and in your own home. No area—and no one—is exempt. Sometimes your instincts help protect you, but at all times, it pays to practice well-thought-out routines to ensure you are doing your reasonable best to avoid situations that may put you in danger or make you a victim of crime.

General Rules

- Stay alert and tuned in to your surroundings. Don't be taken by surprise. Be aware and be prepared.
- Walk confidently. Don't show fear. Don't look like a victim.
- Trust your instincts. If you feel uncomfortable in a place or situation, leave right away, and get help if necessary.
- Choose busy streets and avoid going through vacant

lots, alleys, or other deserted areas. At night, walk in well-lighted areas whenever possible.

- Always lock your car and take the keys, even if you will be gone only a short time.
- If you are coming or going after dark, park in a well-lighted area that will be well lighted when you return.
- Be especially alert when using enclosed parking garages. Don't walk into an area if you feel uncomfortable. Ask a security person to escort you; it's their job.
- Leave only your ignition key with a parking attendant. Don't leave your house key or other keys on the key ring.

ATM Machines

- Plan your ATM visits for during the day.
- Choose an ATM location in a busy public place. Avoid making withdrawals in isolated areas.
- When you finish, place the money in your purse or wallet and leave as soon as possible.
- Watch for suspicious people waiting around an ATM.
- When using a drive-through ATM, keep your doors locked, and be prepared to drive away quickly. If anyone approaches your car on foot, roll up your window and drive away. If you have not finished your transaction, press the "cancel" button, retrieve your card, and leave quickly.

Home and Apartment Safety

- Make sure your home is safe. If you forgot your key, can you get in? If you can, so can a burglar.
- Make sure your windows, especially at ground level, have good locks—and use them.
- Don't tempt burglars. Leaving shades or draperies open helps them spot items of value.
- Make sure porches and other possible entrances are well lighted.
- Never leave a note on the door for anyone explaining why you are not at home.
- Trim any bushes or trees that hide doors or windows.
- Keep ladders, tools, toys, and recreational equipment inside when you are not using them.
- Don't hide your house keys under the doormat or in a flowerpot. It is much wiser to give an extra key to a trusted neighbor.
- Always close and lock garage doors.
- Place only your last name on the mailbox. Never provide marital status or first or middle name on your nameplate or mailbox.
- Ask a trusted neighbor to collect your mail and newspapers when you are traveling and offer to return the favor. Leave word about when you are leaving, when you will return, and how you can be reached in an emergency.
- Put automatic timers on at least two lights and pos-

sibly a radio to help your home look and sound occupied.

- Keep written records of all furniture, jewelry, and electronic products. If possible, keep these records in a safe-deposit box, fireproof safe, or other secure area.
- Replace or re-key locks when moving into an apartment or previously owned home.
- If you live in an apartment, make sure that entrances, parking areas, hallways, stairways, laundry rooms, and other common areas are well lighted. Report burned out bulbs or other problems to the manager.
- Make sure fire stairs are locked from the stairwell side, with an emergency exit at ground level.
- Laundry rooms and storage areas should always be kept locked unless a resident is actually inside.

Telephone Safety

- Never give personal information (e.g., name, age, address) to a stranger on the telephone.
- Never reveal when you will or will not be home or that you are home alone.
- Instruct babysitters never to tell anyone who calls that they are home alone with children.
- Instruct children to say, "My mom can't come to the phone now. May I take a message?" instead of indicating they are home alone.
- If possible, have your calls forwarded while you are out of town, or check your messages regularly.

Car Safety

- As soon as you enter your car, lock the doors. Then get all your items situated and do whatever you need to do sitting in a safe area.
- If you have children, get them in the car and lock the doors. Be aware of your surroundings. Someone could approach your car while you are taking care of the kids and/or adjusting car seats.
- Always lock your car doors while driving and roll windows up far enough to keep anyone from reaching inside.
- At stop signs and lights, keep the car in gear and stay alert.
- Travel well-lighted, busy streets. You can spare the extra minutes it may take to avoid unsafe areas.
- Keep your purse and other valuables out of sight, even when you are driving in your locked car.
- Park in safe, well-lighted areas near your destination.
- When you arrive home, leave your headlights on until you have the car in the garage. Stay in your car and use your remote control garage door opener to lock the garage door. Then exit your car.
- Don't hide spare keys. They can be found.
- If your car breaks down, raise the hood, and place emergency reflectors or flares on the road. Tie a hand-kerchief to the aerial or door handle. Then stay in the locked car. When someone stops to help, don't get

out. Ask him or her, through a closed or cracked window, to telephone the police to come and help. Likewise, if you see a stranded motorist, it is better not to stop. Instead, notify the police.

- If you think you are being followed, do not drive to your home, revealing where you live. Stay calm, think clearly, and control the situation. Flash your lights and sound your horn long enough to attract attention to yourself and, consequently, the person following you. Drive to a fire station, a police station, or a busy, well-lighted retail area—anywhere there will be people and you will feel safe. Continue sounding your horn and flashing your lights. Do not leave the safe location until you are sure the follower is gone. Use your cell phone to call 911.

Rental Cars

- Don't announce that you are a tourist, are driving a rental car, or are totally lost.
- Make sure your rental car is not easily identified as a rental.
- Prepare your route before leaving the rental office or airport lot.
- Invest a little more money to get a car with a global positioning system (GPS) to help prevent your getting lost in an unfamiliar city.
- Try to pick up and return rental cars during daylight hours or when there are people around.

- Keep your luggage in the trunk and your purse/brief-case out of reach and out of sight.
- Always lock the doors and be aware of your surroundings when you get in and out of your car.

Hotel Safety

- Call in advance to ask about the location of the hotel, nearby restaurants, and the surrounding area.
- When you enter a hotel, be aware of your surroundings.
- When you register, keep your personal belongings within your range and view.
- Never leave your credit card out for someone to see your name or credit card numbers.
- Make sure your room number is never given out or announced. The front desk can show you the room number on the folder or key card. If the bellman asks your room number, again just show him. Do not make your room number public. If your room number is given out, ask to change rooms, and tell the clerk not to mention the number.
- Have your room key or card out as you walk to your room. Be ready to enter your room instantly. Never carry so much in your hands that you cannot get into your room quickly.
- Avoid rooms around corners or in dark areas. If you are uncomfortable with the placement of your room, ask to have it changed.
- If there is a sliding door, make sure it has a safety

lock and metal bar. If you are on the first floor and feel uncomfortable, ask to be moved to an upper level.

- The ideal room is between the second and seventh floor, avoiding the ground floor but giving you less distance to cover in case of fire.
- When you enter the room, check the entire area while the bellman is still in the room with you. This includes the closet and the bathroom. You don't have to be obvious, just careful.
- Be aware of the exits on your floor. Make sure the exit doors and routes to them are indicated by illuminated signs.
- Be sure your room has a fire alarm and a sprinkler system.
- Keep your room key and valuables handy in case you need to leave the room quickly.
- Once you are in the room, immediately lock the door, and secure the deadbolt.
- Do not use the latch lock to keep the door open while you run out to get ice or a cold drink. A person could enter your room within that instant.
- Be aware of your surroundings while you are in the hall. If you feel uncomfortable, let hotel security know. Have someone walk you to your room, the parking garage, or your meeting.
- If a room safe is available, use it, or ask the front desk for assistance in securing your valuables.
- When you leave your room, do not put the sign on

your door for the maid to clean your room, announcing that you are out.

- When you leave your room, keep the television or radio on low, and keep a light on for your return. Always give the impression someone is in the room.
- Never leave valuable items out and available in your room.
- Make sure your door closes and locks every time you leave. Some doors will not do that automatically.
- If you order food from outside the hotel, have it delivered to the front desk and have hotel staff deliver it to your room. Do not give out your hotel room number to a stranger or anyone not employed by the hotel.
- If the hotel health club does not have an attendant, use the facility only when there are many people around.
- Use valet parking. It may cost more but it is safer, especially if you arrive late and need to walk through a dark parking lot or garage.

Airline Safety

- Give yourself plenty of time to check in and to go through security points, due to the heightened security precautions at airports.
- Time recommendations will vary but most airports suggest you arrive ninety minutes before domestic flight departures when you are checking your luggage and sixty minutes before departure if you will have only

carry-ons. For international flights, travelers are advised to arrive no less than two hours before departure.

- For all flights it is necessary to have a government-issued photo ID available as well as your ticket or printed itinerary for electronic ticketing.
- Photo identification is sometimes required at both check-in and boarding. Minors must be verified by a parent or guardian.
- For flying internationally, passports, visas, and inoculation information are necessary.
- If you have a very early morning flight, confirm the ticket counter opening time with the airport to prevent unnecessary waiting.

Airport Security Checkpoints

- Be prepared to have all your carry-on items completely examined. This procedure can take three or four times longer than previous security checks. New procedures are in place for your safety and the safety of all passengers, so please remember this when security personnel ask you to remove your shoes or boots or to go back through a check point.
- Do not expect any wrapped gifts to go through security. They will be subject to search so don't bother with wrapping.
- At security or boarding, your bags may be subjected to a random search or you may have to submit to an electronic wand search.

- Do not leave your bags unattended or ask anyone to watch your bags.

In Flight

- Many people now have concerns about flying and new security procedures have been implemented. The airlines and airports are doing everything possible to provide a comfortable and safe experience.
- If you have a concern or are alarmed about a passenger(s), immediately notify a flight attendant.
- Recent safety studies recommend verbally confronting a violent, unusual, or combative person before attempting to restrain him.
- Do not take it upon yourself to be a hero or react hastily. In any situation, on the ground or in the air, use the best resources you have available before trying to handle a situation on your own. There are now personnel on planes and on the ground who have been trained for these circumstances.

THE POINT IS . . .
Always be alert and aware of your surroundings.

TWELVE

Tipping Guidelines

● ● ● ● ● ● ●

Many service people receive more from gratuities than they are paid in actual salary. Tip according to the services they provide. You may write a tip on your bill and charge the total to your credit card or hotel room. You should always be prepared with smaller bills when traveling. But if you have insufficient cash, you may ask the person you wish to tip if he has change. If you promise to take care of someone later, make sure to honor that commitment when you have proper change.

Hotels

- BELLMAN: If one person carries your luggage from the car or taxi to the registration desk, waits for you, and then carries the bags to your room, he should receive no less than $1; $3 to $4 for several bags. It is more likely that one person will carry your bags from the car to the front desk and a second person will escort you to your room. If this is the case, both should be tipped. My guideline is $2 for the first bag and $1 for each additional bag. It does become costly when several bellmen are involved. Think ahead and put a few dollars in your pocket or someplace easy to access quickly, so you won't expose the contents of your wallet in the hotel lobby.

- CONCIERGE: Just asking a small request of a concierge does not require a tip. But if a concierge performs a special service, such as getting you tickets to the theater or a dinner reservation at the newest restaurant in town, tip $5 to $10 or more if the request took a long time or was difficult to accomplish.

- DOORMAN: If this person quickly gets you a cab, you may want to tip from $1 to $5, depending on the weather and the number of guests waiting in line. If you arrive at a hotel and ask the doorman to hold your car up front while you go in for lunch or a meeting, then $5 to $10 is appropriate.

- MAID: A $1 to $2 per day gratuity can be left in a marked envelope on the nightstand, near the bathroom sink, or on the bed. You should leave these tips on a daily basis because of shift changes. Envelopes usually can be found in the hotel's guest directory folder. If an envelope is not available, then just leave the money with a brief thank-you note on the bed.

- PARKING GARAGE ATTENDANT: $1 to $2

- RESTROOM ATTENDANTS: Tip $.50 to $1

- SHOE SHINE: $1 to $2

- SPA ATTENDANT: Tip $2 if he or she provides towels or services.

- VALET: Charges for valet services will appear on the

room bill, but $1 (more if you have more items serviced) is a good delivery tip.

- VALET PARKING: $1 to $2 is normal. If the valet holds your car in the front of the building for a brief time, then $5 to $10 is appropriate.

Restaurants

- At a modest restaurant, 15 percent is a good guideline; 20 percent to 25 percent at a more expensive restaurant is standard.

- The maitre d' usually is not tipped, but if you are a regular at the restaurant or if he provides you with a great table or helps you with a very important business meal, then $5 to $20 is appropriate.

- The captain or head waiter should be tipped 5 percent of the bill. This can be either in cash or specified on the bill if you use a credit card.

- Servers should be tipped approximately 15 percent to 20 percent of your total bill, according to the level of service provided. Usually this tip is divided among the entire service team, including bartenders and bussing staff.

- The sommelier (wine steward) should be tipped 15 percent of the wine bill. But this is necessary only if the sommelier performs a special service for you and your guests by selecting or assisting with the wine choices for your meal.

- European tipping: It is the custom in most European countries to include the tip, or a gratuity of usually 15 percent, in the restaurant bill before it is presented. If the service is extraordinary, you can provide an additional tip.

Other Tipping

- BARBERS, HAIR STYLISTS, MASSEURS AND MANICURISTS: A tip equivalent to 15 percent to 20 percent of the cost of the service is customary.
- CAB DRIVERS: The usual tip is 15 percent to 20 percent of your fare on the meter, plus $1 per bag if the driver loads them in and out of the trunk.
- CHECK ROOM ATTENDANTS: $1 per coat. Add another dollar for a briefcase, umbrella, or any other item.
- DELIVERY PERSONS: People who deliver flowers, groceries (whether to your door or your car), meals, fruit baskets, etc., should be tipped $1 to $3, depending on the number or weight and size of the items. Federal Express, DHL, UPS and U.S. Postal Service delivery people are not usually tipped, but a $10 to $20 holiday tip for the regular service provider is appropriate. Trash collectors, newspaper deliverymen, yardmen, maids, and other service suppliers may also receive annual holiday gratuities.
- FAST FOOD RESTAURANTS: The wait staff that cleans up after your child's birthday party at a fast-food chain or pizza parlor or a person who is standing on the corner in the heat to serve you a hot dog or ice cream deserves a $1 to $3 tip.

- GOLF CADDIE: Tip 15 percent to 20 percent of the price of the green fee.
- LUGGAGE HANDLERS AT AIRPORTS OR TRAIN STATIONS: At least $1 per checked bag is paid when you receive the claim checks.

THE POINT IS . . .

Carry enough small bills for tipping the service people who assist you, and don't forget to request some smaller bills when exchanging currency for international trips.

THIRTEEN

Business Entertainment, Gifts, and RSVPs

● ● ● ● ● ● ● ●

Business entertaining can range from a one-on-one luncheon to programs, sporting events, or meetings for hundreds of people. The intent when you entertain may be to meet someone for the first time, close a business deal, strengthen a business relationship, or sell clients on your company and what you can offer them. If at the end of each function you believe your goal was accomplished, then it was worth your time, your money, and the time of your customers.

Individual Entertainment

Even a dinner for one client needs research. You can check with a client's assistant to learn about a favorite restaurant and food or wine preferences. Planning will be appreciated by the client and can make a difference for you and your business.

On a one-on-one basis, you may entertain to:
- Introduce yourself to the client
- Thank someone for a great job or for their business

- Promote your company and products
- Exchange ideas
- Honor an individual or a group on a special occasion

Group Entertainment

Detailed planning is involved when entertaining groups to showcase your organization or product. Every detail must be covered to make your event a complete success. To get the most from your investment, you must know your audience.

For a two- or three-day event, your planning may include:
- Activities/Tickets (plays, concerts, sporting events)
- Amenities
- Back-up venues for any outside activities
- Budget
- Entertainment (unique, creative, and different)
- Flowers/Decorations
- Hotel/Venues
- Invitations/RSVPs
- Itinerary
- Menus (no duplicates during the event)
- Photographers/Videographers
- Press
- Security (if needed)
- Sponsors
- Staffing
- Transportation (both air and ground)

Make sure your guests know:

- The complete itinerary you have planned
- The dress code for each part of the event
- If they may bring a guest. If so, be extremely specific about the details.
- Airline details (cancellation/change policies and deadlines)
- That the invitation is nontransferable

Bringing an Extra Person

Never bring a date or a friend to an event or dinner party unless the invitation clearly states "and guest." Especially in the situation of a dinner party, the hosts probably have set only for the invited guests who responded. For you to show up with a guest would be extremely uncomfortable for everyone. Children should not be included at a business event unless specifically designated.

Paying the Bill

- If you invite someone to a luncheon or dinner, you should pick up the bill. As soon as the bill arrives, move it to your side of the table, and handle it immediately so there is no confusion or argument over who pays.
- If two business acquaintances frequently dine together as friends, even though some business is discussed, it is perfectly fine to split the bill or take turns picking up the bill.

- If a woman invites a man or several men to lunch to discuss her new project or a business deal, it is appropriate that she pay the bill. It is best that she handles payment ahead of time with the headwaiter or restaurant manager. Then her guests will never see the bill, and there will be no discussion.

Arriving for a Business Function

- Punctuality is critical for all business meetings. You should make every effort to arrive a few minutes early. If you arrive ahead of your guest at a restaurant, you should wait a few minutes before going in to sit alone. If you see the restaurant is getting crowded, you may ask to be seated unless the restaurant has a policy of seating only complete parties.
- If several people are invited to lunch, ask to be seated as soon as two people have arrived assuming the restaurant will accommodate you.
- If you are waiting at the table or a bar for another person or persons, it is completely acceptable to order a beverage before the other person arrives, but you should never order your meal before your guests arrive.

Business Gifts

Sometimes it is difficult to determine when we should give gifts to clients, coworkers, or a boss. You don't want to seem to be bribing your clients, buying your way into a particular group at work, or looking for a promotion from your boss. But it is thoughtful to thank people for their help or service, or for introducing you to a new client, and to congratulate clients or coworkers on special occasions or at the completion of a successful project. Whatever the situation, your gift should be sincere, well thought out, and within your budget.

Be aware of how others may react to your gift. If your company is cutting back on expenditures and possibly even downsizing, spend your gift budget cautiously and appropriately.

No Gifts Please

For a retirement party or a party to honor an important associate or client, putting "No gifts, please" on an invitation sends a negative connotation. A gentler way of declining gifts is to explain it when the guests RSVP. Still, some guests may want to bring gifts to show their appreciation. If gifts are received, they should not be opened at the party. If you wish to give a gift, send it to the honoree before or after the event.

Give-aways/Amenities

Promotional products are given away at trade shows and are available to sales teams to leave with clients. You can spend from $1 or less to $100 or more on promotional gifts, depending on whether you distribute them to hundreds at a trade show or give them individually to top clients.

Display your company logo on your items, but place it discreetly because some people may choose not to wear or use your gift if the logo is too large. Be a little less conspicuous if you want to see people carrying around the bags you gave them or wearing your jacket year after year.

Choosing and Presenting Gifts

- The best gifts are ones that are chosen with the recipient in mind. Know your clients and staff and give appropriate gifts. It makes no sense to give a box of golf balls to a nongolfer or a plant to someone who has a "brown thumb."
- If a woman is sending a male coworker a gift, she should send the gift to his office with a note. But if she was invited to his home, she should send the flowers or gift to his home addressed to both his wife and him.
- Send flowers the following day as a thank-you instead of bringing them the night of a party. Chances are the host has already decorated the home and needs to concentrate on the meal and the guests, rather than to stop and find a vase to display your gift. Flowers arriving the next morning would show appreciation for the host's work.
- If you bring wine to a party don't expect your hosts to

open the wine and drink it that night. It is a gift for them to enjoy after the party.

- If you are sending flowers or perishable gifts, make sure the recipients are home or in the office to accept them. Sending food to the office is always good. It can and should be shared with coworkers.

- Liquor is also a good gift, but make sure the recipient drinks and prefers the type of alcohol you select. Someone who does not drink could be offended by a gift of alcohol. (If you send vodka to someone who drinks only gin, it will be obvious that you did not research your gift.)

- Gift certificates are great. Although they may seem a little less personal, if you choose a service or product tailored to the tastes or interests of the recipient, gift certificates will be appreciated.

- Be aware if a client or company can, in fact, receive gifts. Some company and government policies do not allow employees to accept gifts above a specified value.

- Receiving a gift does not mean you have to give one in return. There are times when people simply want to show their appreciation. Accept the gift, be happy that they thought to buy you one, and send a thank-you note.

- Executive staff may be invited to everything. As an executive, you do not have to attend each celebration or send a gift, but a handwritten note would be appropriate.

- You can give your boss a gift, but it would be difficult for the boss to give everyone in his or her company a gift in return. Your gift should be from the heart and could even be homemade cookies or something simple to express your appreciation.

- Most offices do not have rules and regulations about giving gifts among coworkers. Use your good judgment in deciding whether to give gifts or in selecting appropriate gifts for anniversaries, weddings, baby showers, and other occasions.
- Secretary Week is a good time to thank your assistants for their work all year round. Such gifts can be from you individually or from the company.

Thank-you Notes

Send thank-you notes promptly to show your appreciation. If you receive a gift from a company or a department, send the note to the president or the head of the department. If ten people send you one gift, all contributing and signing their names, you should send a thank you note to each of them.

When you send a thank-you note, be sure to mention the gift, how much you enjoy it or appreciate it, and how you are going to use it. It makes the person who gave the gift feel it is appreciated.

Responding to an RSVP

- It is the height of rudeness not to respond to the host of your intention to accept or decline an invitation.

- Reply within one week to a request for response. Whether or not you plan to attend, it is still very important to respond.
- If you accepted an invitation and discover at the last minute you cannot attend, make every effort to contact the host the day of the event or the next day. The following are other options:
  - Call the location of the event and speak with the general manager, maitre d' or the hotel banquet manager and insist your message be passed to the host. You don't have to talk to the host personally, but make sure the message is given.
  - Write a note to the host the next day explaining your "no-show."
  - Call the host the next day to explain and apologize.
  - If you are called out of town on business, send an apology from that city, and call when you return.
  - Never bring a guest without calling first to ask the host. Offer to pay for your guest. In business settings, it may be inappropriate to bring an uninvolved person to a dinner/event.
  - Be on time. Don't arrive at 7:40 PM for an event that was scheduled from 6:30 PM to 8:00 PM.

Extending Invitations with RSVPs

- R.S.V.P., RSVP, or R.s.v.p. are all correct.
- A deadline for RSVP may be given.
- To facilitate responses, be sure to give guest's a phone,

fax and/or e-mail contact with names and numbers, or include a self-addressed card and postage.

- "Acceptance only" and "regrets only" rarely are effective in giving the host an accurate guest count, although one would expect them to work as well as RSVP. You can almost calculate that two-thirds of your list will actually show. If it is a rainy, stormy day, subtract as much as half from the list, and you will probably have a fairly accurate count.

THE POINT IS . . .
The best business entertainment and gifts result from knowing your clients. Common courtesy requires a response to every RSVP.

Reading List

● ● ● ● ● ● ●

Letitia Baldridge. *Letitia Baldridge's New Complete Guide to Executive Manners.* Scribner. 1993.

Susan Bixler and Nancy Nix-Rice. *The New Professional Image from Business Casual to the Ultimate Power Look.* Adams Media Corp. 1997.

Laurie D. Borman. *The Smart Woman's Guide to Business Travel.* Career Press. 1999.

Laurel Cardone. *Fodor's How-to-Pack Experts Share Their Secrets.* Fodor's Travel Publications. 1997.

Lisa Kanarek. *Organizing Your Home Office for Success.* Penguin-Plume. 1993.

Mary Mitchell with John Corr. *The Complete Idiot's Guide to Business Etiquette.* Alpha Books. 1999.

Barbara Pachter and Marjorie Brody with Betsy Anderson. *Prentice Hall Complete Business Etiquette Handbook.* Prentice Hall Press. 1994.

Linda and Wayne Phillips. *The Concise Guide to Executive Etiquette.* Doubleday. 1990.

Peggy Post. *Emily Post's Etiquette, 16th Edition.* Harper Collins. 1997.

Karyn Repinski. *The Complete Idiot's Guide to Successful Dressing.* Alpha Books. 1999.

Ann Marie Sabath. *Business Etiquette: 101 Ways to Conduct Business with Charm and Savvy.* Career Press. 1997.

Nat Segaloff. *The Everything Etiquette Book.* Adams Media Corp. 1997.

Colleen A. Rickenbacher, CMP, CSEP

● ● ● ● ● ● ●

A native of Pennsylvania, Colleen Rickenbacher served the Dallas Convention & Visitors Bureau for fifteen years as vice president of event planning. She continues to work with the Dallas CVB as a contract event planner, but in 2001 started her own company, Colleen Rickenbacher Inc., as an independent event planner and speaker.

Over the past ten years, Rickenbacher has had numerous speaking engagements including a seminar for the Certified Meeting Professional teaching program in Florence, Italy, a guest lecture at Cornell University School of Hotel Administration in New York, and a presentation about customer service to 150 government and city officials in Zimbabwe, Africa.

Rickenbacher's speaking topics include Business and Dining Etiquette, Working Out of Your Home, How to Add the "Wow!" to Your Next Event, Dressing Professionally, Safety at Home and on the Road, Packing Tips for Business Trips, Serving Your Clients, and Networking: How to Work a Room.

Rickenbacher is past chair of the Certified Meeting Professional Board of the Convention Industry Council. She serves on the board of directors of Meeting Professionals International (MPI) and is a past president of the MPI Dallas/Fort Worth chapter. Rickenbacher was the first president of the Texas chapter of the Association for Convention Operations Management. She has been an advisory board member of the International Special Events Society.

An award-winning event planner, Rickenbacher earned a BS in business administration with a minor in international business from Northwood University. She holds the designations of Certified Meeting Professional (CMP) and Certified Special Events Professional (CSEP). Rickenbacher was recognized as the "1999 Meeting Partner of the Year" by the National Speakers Association and received the 1999 Marion N. Kershner Award from MPI for motivational leadership. The Colleen Rickenbacher Leadership Award, created in her honor, annually recognizes an outstanding leader from the MPI Dallas/Fort Worth chapter.

Rickenbacher and her husband, Steve, reside in Dallas. They have three children. Son Jon lives in St. Petersburg Beach, Florida; daughter Lauren lives in Nashville, Tennessee with her husband Jackson; daughter Andrea and her husband Steven also reside in Dallas, with their son Shaeffer.

VISIT THE AUTHOR'S WEB SITE AT
www.colleenrickenbacher.com.